IT'S ME VS ME

R GANZEL AND MJ CUTSINGER

Terra Theoria Publishing LLC
www.terratheoria.com

ISBN: 979-8-9987795-7-2

Library of Congress Control Number: 2025909916

Disclaimer:

This book is not intended as a substitute for professional medical or

psychological advice. Consult health practitioners regarding physical,

mental, or emotional health and any symptoms needing diagnosis or

treatment. We are not doctors and hold no certifications.

Published by: Terra Theoria Publishing LLC

www.terratheoria.com

Table of Contents

Acknowledgements

I would like to dedicate this book to my family and friends; without your unwavering support and encouragement it could have stayed in the box. And a special thanks to the captain of my blanket fort, you remain a light in the darkest of tunnels. –R Ganzel

I would like to dedicate this book to my family and friends; you all have been awesome cheerleaders through my journey. I wish to give a special dedication to every reader, thank you for giving these words a place to land. You are the dreamers, doers, and silent fighters who never give up on what matters most. Keep going, your story is still unfolding, and is also worth telling. –MJ Cutsinger

Figure 1: MJ sitting on the peak of Huayna Picchu overlooking Machu Picchu.

One can only wonder what is going through her mind at this very moment!

Chapter 1

A Vision of What Life Could Be Like

"Several years ago, a surgeon had to reattach both of my feet after I shattered my ankles. Two metal plates, sixteen screws, three pins, and eighteen-gauge wire later, I was left bedridden for a year. Imagine me today, literally climbing mountains in the clouds."–
MJ Cutsinger

Imagine being able to walk or run through an entire theme park like Universal Studios Orlando or Islands of Adventure and riding every roller coaster even in your fifties. **Imagine** having the ability to do things you love and things that excite you without being hampered by the limitations of your body because of weight.

For a long time now, I have taken certain things for granted, like the ability to go to a public beach and rent a chair. You've seen those chairs; they look like a handful of toothpicks propping up a towel and what about being able to get down and up from them without assistance?

How do you feel about bathing suits? Do you love your clothes or would you like having different sizes and places to shop for fashions you want? Imagine dressing as you like without paying extra for adjustments or shopping at stores that cater to larger sizes.

Surprisingly, weight can impact your choices in shoes, ties, socks, underwear, bras, and even suspenders. Now **Imagine** taking an entire closet full of your old clothes and dropping them off for donations because they've become too large for you.

Imagine taking significantly less or even none of your medications. MJ managed hypertension, diabetes, a thyroid disorder, and other health issues with thirteen medications over twenty-five years. Her dietary changes have now resolved most of these conditions.

Think of the money she can and does save, the money you could save. (1) In 2018, the American Diabetes Association and the Heart Association reported diabetes and hypertension combined, cost about eighteen thousand dollars per person annually. I imagine the costs have only gotten higher and will keep rising.

We also invite you to **imagine** less pain with vastly improved mobility, even for simple things like getting in and out of a bathtub. Maybe you'll take a seat on the ground or on a backpack while you wait in line at theme parks and then get back up with nothing but a helping hand. These are all things most people don't think about and just do. These abilities are easily taken for granted and MJ brought this home to my attention when she said,

"It is hugely different from having to roll off the recliner onto the floor and then crawl to your dog. People who are physically able overlook the ease of getting down and up from the ground in one swift motion, rather than several awkward attempts."

She recalls with clarity the day she comfortably fits into an airplane seat without encroaching on other passengers' space. There are so many little things you can change that will cascade into bigger changes and make huge impacts on your health, wealth and well-being. It can even change your sex life and create more intimacy.

With this book, MJ and I are inviting you to share our memories and experiences during MJ's life transformation and her realization of exciting, lifetime goals. We include transcripts from our recorded journals and hope you find them engaging and natural so you may **imagine** and share in joy with us.

We don't want to keep you waiting, let's get right to the exciting parts as MJ recounts our experience at Universal Orlando during my birthday celebration. One hundred pounds lighter, MJ would be getting on the first roller coaster of her life.

Figure 2: MJ 1 year later in front of the raptor experience Universal Studios Orlando.

Who's Mummy is it?

Transcripts Audio Journal

"It is not down in any map; true places never are."–

Moby Dick by Herman Melvilles

RENEE: Last week, we were at universal with the kids, and we walked straight to the mummy. I made Molly stand in front of the test chair and I told her your story.

"OK this is it," I told her. "This is where it happened for MJ, and she was so scared. She had never been on a roller coaster before, like ever! She was big her whole life and couldn't fit in any safety restraints or even the newer, modified seats they have now. She always had to wait on the sidelines holding cups and bags."

I explained to Molly how I wanted you to come for my birthday celebration and I was sure you had made enough progress to get on the coasters.

As we stood in front of The Mummy test chair, I felt Molly was impressed and kind of touched. I also told her about the ride operator who was with us at the bottom of the line supervising the entrance.

MJ: Did you tell her how she took us to the top of the line and put us in the very front seat right there in front of everyone?

RENEE: Yes! I couldn't do it justice though because it wasn't you telling the story. What do you remember most about that first day? Would you say it was being able to walk straight through the turnstile like everyone else or sitting in the Mummy chair? What kind of feelings did you have when you approached the Mummy Coaster? You were walking extra slow and later you told me you were stalling; you were terrified you wouldn't fit, and it would feel awful.

MJ: I was so terrified.

RENEE: Do you still worry every time we approach it? Do you like, slip back in time in your mind and fear not fitting?

MJ: Not so much.

RENEE: Good. So, walk us through it. We met, I came to your place, we hung out at your house for the night and then we went to Orlando the next morning. On the drive, you got us lost for 45 minutes!

"Oh, we'll be there in just a few minutes," you kept saying, and then 45 minutes later you were like, "Oh hell we're going the wrong direction."

MJ: Right but–

RENEE: Yeah, I think you subconsciously were trying to put it off.

MJ: I was really working through some heavy things in my mind.

RENEE: What kind of things?

MJ: I was afraid I wouldn't fit, the fear of disappointment and just… a lot of fear.

RENEE: How did you get through it all? While you were hanging back, going so painfully slow, I had to keep checking behind me and I felt like I was pushing you. I kept saying,

"Come on, come on!" Finally, you came and stood in front of the Mummy's test chair. I wish I could say what was on your face but, I was so focused on the test chair and my own fears for you I saw little else. I think I was trying to will the latch to click and the light to turn green. I knew it might be close but, damn it, if my willpower could give you an extra half inch then I would stare it into existence! *(Long moment of silence as we sat in memory)*

RENEE: When I told you to get in the test chair, didn't you tell me something like,

"Yeah, let's go somewhere else first. We're not doing this yet."?

MJ: I did.

RENEE: I responded vehemently,

"No! We're not leaving this spot until you get in that chair."

MJ: Anyways, after a little positive affirmation from you, I took a deep breath and positioned myself into the seat. You proceeded to pull the harness and bar down over the top of me.

RENEE: I did?

MJ: Yes ma'am, and you didn't stop till the belt latched!

RENEE: Oh, but come on now, you make it sound like we forced it! It actually went pretty easy.

MJ: Felt like it wasn't gonna go easy, I don't know, some adjusting, not much but a little.

RENEE: You know what I remember, I remember the look on your face when the buckle clicked, and the light turned green. At first it looked like complete and utter disbelief. You scared me for a minute because I watched your face fall, and you just started losing it. You were crying.

MJ: Yup. *(Heavy sigh.)*

RENEE: Are you getting emotional now?

MJ: Yeah.

RENEE: Yeah, a hard moment to share.

MJ: Yeah. *(We had to take a minute here because we both became too emotional)*

RENEE: Only now do I imagine how difficult these moments were for you. I failed to anticipate your level of fear and anxiety and I'm ashamed to say, I didn't take any of that into consideration. Your hesitancy, your fear did not cross my mind, and I feel like maybe I wasn't cognizant of what you were going through.

MJ: You were just what I needed.

RENEE: So, what happened after you started bawling? Do you remember? *(Long pause full of Crickets.)*

Do you want me to go on for you?

MJ: Yeah.

RENEE: At the base where the line forms for the mummy, you're sitting in the test cart bawling your eyes out and the girl, the employee, turns around and she's freaking out and probably worried thinking —

MJ: She probably thought, "Oh God we have a loose one!"

(Pause for laughter and jokes. Some of them would be in poor taste to others.)

RENEE: She asks if you're okay. You were too busy crying, so I said, "Yeah, she's fine." Then I told her about your weight loss journey and how this was your first time ever on a roller coaster. I said you were just feeling overwhelmed because it was your lifelong goal to be able to ride the mummy and she did it. Look! She fits! I mentioned it's my birthday too, so it's a gift for me as well.

"Oh my God!" She gushes and claps her hands.
She gives us each one of those special necklaces. You know, the mummy necklaces you normally have to buy in the gift shop...

MJ: That we still have.

RENEE: Yeah, you and I still have hanging in my jeep for protection because it's the eye of Rah or something and it's supposed to be protective. So, she gives us each one and she's like,

"Well, this deserves something special," She walks us around the back of the ride and up the exit ramp, leading us to the head of the line to go next in the front row.

MJ: She then made an announcement over the PA system in the control room, making sure everyone waiting for the ride understood why this experience was significant for me.

RENEE: After asking us of course, and the whole place, everyone who was at the top of the line in the launch room started clapping for you.

MJ: Oh my god yes! Everyone was clapping all around me. There were strangers being happy for me, patting me on my shoulders through the headrests of the coaster behind me. People were cheering and congratulating me, and it was all very moving. I cried some more.

RENEE: I looked at you and I said,

"Well thanks for the world's most awesome birthday present ever in my life."

I remember you were nervous about entering the park because of the turnstiles. I believe they were your very first boost in confidence.

13

You waltzed right through them with a HUGE smile. I think you did an extra spin just for the hell of it because you finally could didn't you?

MJ: Probably, yeah. I hope I did because they're gone now. Honestly those two moments are fastened together in my mind forever.

RENEE: I also had mentioned this to Molly, how you would go to universal with your family and be terribly embarrassed because you couldn't get into the park through the turnstiles. They had those big, metal, revolving ones you walk around inside of. They look like two giant metal combs sliding through each other like gears.

MJ: It spins, and the poles slide over and under each other and you gotta walk through it. Well, I was too big and couldn't fit. I had to step in sideways and shuffle through them. I even got stuck one time.

RENEE: Yeah, yeah. *(We both had to sit in silence for a minute because the memory never loses power to move us.)*

MJ: I can't even begin to tell you what emotions were running through me. It was crazy because I had negative emotions too. I was afraid of letting you down, I was afraid of letting myself down.

RENEE: I understand. Once you realized you could ride the roller coaster and we actually got in the front row, were you terrified of the roller coaster?

MJ: Absolutely not. I was terrified of what I had going through my mind and about my future! I had gained this much momentum, and I knew I had to keep going forward from this point on. I had the determination I just didn't know if I was strong enough for it. Clearly, I was. I'm still going!

RENEE: So, wow, you know, there's something not getting enough airtime. Once you've started to succeed and once you've begun to get close to goals, you can feel a whole new set of fears you must address because they can sabotage you if you don't.

MJ: Yeah. One day at a time, I guess.

RENEE: For now, let's do twelve hours at a time. Twelve hours at a time is a great way to manage habit-changing and weight loss.

MJ: You get set in certain ways and you know you have habits to change, and I mean my habits changed…

RENEE: But you didn't feel like they were drastic because they seemed so gradual yeah?

MJ: Don't get me wrong. When I say habits changed dramatically, I don't mean diet wise going balls to the walls. There were changes in my diet, but they were gradual, and I didn't miss them so much when the changes were making me feel better. Anyway, I think a lot of the mummy was mental.

RENEE: Yeah, you will be challenged mentally, everywhere, all the time. More so than I realized apparently. I failed to consider your fears and anxieties because I wrongly assumed you would be too filled with excitement.

MJ: It was a beautiful day. I am sorry I didn't share with you more but, it was a terrifying walk at times.

RENEE: Well, how was your first roller coaster experience? Did the mummy itself scare you?

MJ: Well, it wasn't scary. It takes quite a bit to scare me.

RENEE: Yeah no, the mummy's kind of a wussy coaster.

MJ: Ask Skyler. Skyler didn't think it was for wussies!

RENEE: *(Laughing hard)* You told Skyler,

15

"This ride is for babies, really and it's rather gentle actually. I don't even know what we're doing on it."

MJ: Yeah, then all of a sudden,

"Oh my god!" He screamed and screamed. He got me back later that day though.

RENEE: What was next on the list, the Velocicoaster?

MJ: Oh my. We waited in line forever, right?

RENEE: We did, and you were able to stand in these crazy lines all day. That's another thing, not only could you run around the park all day long, but you were also able to stand in the lines.

MJ: Right, because you can't sit on their walls that's for damn sure!

RENEE: Oh, don't you sit on those walls! You'll be removed from the park.

MJ: Standing in line for an hour and a half, maybe two while waiting for the very front seat was a challenge by then. My arthritis was kicking, but my adrenaline was high, and I wasn't gonna let pain stop this perfect day.

RENEE: Your adrenaline ramped up while waiting in line for Velocicoaster?

MJ: Yes, because it looked much more intense than The Mummy. When we eventually got on, the seats and harness were nice and snug, and I felt secure and everything. It was pretty thrilling and–

RENEE: We were in the front row of course.

MJ: I know you were waiting for me to holler out like a scared little kid, but I didn't give you the satisfaction.

RENEE: I was a little disappointed I didn't get to hear you wailing.

MJ: Yeah, I took it all in. A lot of our first day was taking it all in.

RENEE: I bet it almost felt–

MJ: Euphoric.

RENEE: Maybe even a little surreal?

MJ: Yeah.

RENEE: It was like you weren't quite there?

MJ: In fact, I asked you once or twice to pinch me.

RENEE: A couple of times you were like,

> "Is this really happening?" I kept cheering you on.
>
> "Yeah, you're really doing it!"

MJ: We discussed different things and really talked about our journey a lot. Then from the Velocicoaster, we went over to the Hulk. Going through the metal detectors in line was kind of a bad moment for me when it kept alerting to the metal in my body. I had a melt down on the ride operator. I didn't get us kicked out at least.

RENEE: You were under a lot of pressure even though it was fun, it was still a pressure you weren't used to.

MJ: I wasn't used to it because I've never been able to be in line for it.

RENEE: Exactly! So, there's all kinds of new experiences as well as new pressure.

MJ: We did end up getting on the Hulk after about an hour wait, and I enjoyed the hell out of it as well. We had quite the workout.

RENEE: We did.

MJ: I also had a lot to absorb. By the time we were standing in line at Gringotts, I was leaning heavily on you and getting tired but, I went back and finished off our night on the Velocicoaster. Night riding the Velocicoaster is quite a different experience.

RENEE: What about when we went back the following year for my next birthday?

MJ: Oh yeah, a whole different experience too!

RENEE: A whole different experience you say? Talk about it a little bit.

MJ: Well, the first time we went, I still weighed two hundred and forty-five pounds. Remember, I started this journey at three hundred and forty-eight, so I had already lost one hundred pounds. Well, in the second year, this past year, I was down to one hundred and ninety.

(A long pause and a look passes over MJ's face; I look at her questioning...)

MJ: Yeah, I just had a moment.

RENEE: I know. I'm sitting here looking at your face right now and you had a hard time with that.

MJ: So almost another one hundred pounds? Well let's do the math, *(348-190= 158)* pounds in a year and a half.

RENEE: Think this stuff works?

MJ: This works! At three hundred and forty-eight pounds I couldn't get on the ride at all. At two hundred and forty-eight pounds I got on the rides, but I still had enough bulk to fit very snug in the seats under the safety harnesses.

RENEE: Yeah, you were strapped in pretty secure. You fit but, it was such a close fit the first time.

MJ: So, I was in there snug as a bug and I wasn't shifting around in the seat the first time. The experience I was getting was—

RENEE: Only the coaster movement.

MJ: Yeah. This time I could feel a new kind of fear and thrill. The whole thing was so different now with even more weight lost, I had room to slide around under my harness. I would shift around in the chairs and come up off the seats!

RENEE: You were so much lighter and smaller in the chair. When we went through the loops and over drops, I sensed your shock at feeling your body come up off the chair for the first time, you almost screamed. It came out as a scary squeak or something like,

"Oh shit that's scary!"

MJ: I did something on the Velocicoaster I hadn't done in quite a few years.

RENEE: Scream like a banshee?

MJ: Well, besides screaming, I was able to take my legs and wrap them around the bottom of the seat and squeeze tight. It's kind of like squeezing around a horse when you want it to go faster. I'm surprised I didn't have leg cramps that night. In fact, I think I did.

RENEE: You couldn't ever cross your legs before?

MJ: No, and now I could, and I did because it scared me. I thought I was gonna fall out.

RENEE: How many times did we ride before you realized you're not actually gonna fall out and you could stop squeezing?

MJ: I still squeeze.

RENEE: Are you feeling a difference still, every time we go and you're down several more pounds?

MJ: This past month I did, yes.

RENEE: What was the difference last month?

MJ: I move around even more. You know on the Velocicoaster when you go upside down in a corkscrew over the pond? I actually dangled upside down this time and my weight shifted from my butt to my shoulders. My stomach slipped up too because the only thing holding me in now are the harnesses. That's how it feels all the time now because I have such a smaller mass, no more bulk, I guess.

RENEE: Right! When it whips you upside down you think you're going in the water.

MJ: On the Hulk after it cranks up, the lights are all going and it suddenly shoots you up into open sky, only to immediately jerk you towards the ground through an upside-down corkscrew roll. It pulled my ass right off the seat! There I was, forced up against the bars holding me in thinking, wow alright, I didn't get THAT experience the first time! So, it was all brand new to me again. Each time we go it's a new experience.

RENEE: It's a new you every time, so you get a new experience every time.

MJ: Very good. I really look forward to more of this feeling. I'd even like to try some of those little parks in Gatlinburg.

RENEE: Or stuff with maybe one intense roller coaster, not horribly bouncy and you know, ones that don't jack us up for a week. Many coasters may look like a smooth ride but, when you have joint and spinal conditions, the signs in the park mean what they say.

MJ: Yeah, I will say with this enormous loss of weight, I get jerked around a lot more.

RENEE: And sometimes it's not always fabulous getting older. It sucks a little bit.

MJ: But you know, again with me, it comes down to something else you helped me understand. You gotta keep the body in motion, and I've known this. Considering I have Rheumatoid Arthritis, I've known I gotta keep moving if I wanna keep my joint's mobility.

My food choices and movement are definitely a thing a lot of people skipped over and never discussed with me, so I never really considered it. You've gotta try really hard to maintain whatever motion you've still got and maybe even try to push through therapeutic movements to regain lost abilities. A body in motion you gotta be.

RENEE: You and I both always hurt, make no mistake about it. Sometimes we cry ourselves to sleep and take a bunch of anti-inflammatories or other plant medicines to feel better. We try to stay away from pharmaceuticals.

MJ & RENEE: *(In perfect sync again)* Au' naturelle' and green.

MJ: A nice hot tub does wonders. Depending on what the day has been like, I may pop the top off a beer occasionally now.

RENEE: This kind of fun has a higher price to be paid when you're older and have autoimmune situations. We're not the same for the next month and we can barely bend over to tie our shoes. We may have to go visit our doctor for cortisone shots when the adrenaline wears off but, boy what a rush!

MJ: I feel as if our stamina is getting stronger as each day goes by. I believe we've both experienced significant improvements with our issues. I know I have since losing so much weight and like you said, living cleanly as possible as a lifestyle.

You know, I still have debilitating pain as do you but, there have definitely been some improvements making life with my condition not so depressing. I'm doing, I'm moving, I'm trying things which hurt like hell. It's better than letting my condition take everything from me and

21

just growing bigger and bigger on a couch somewhere while waiting and wanting to die. Because that's where I was.

Now, I couldn't count the miles we kayaked, walked, and we played. We hurt and we cried, and we need a lot of time to recover afterwards, but at least we're living a bit.

End of Transcript

Figure 3: Kayaking a river outside of Dallas Texas with Renee and Jen.

Adventure is now welcomed into MJ's life!

Figure 4: MJ before and after around 8 months into her journey.

Chapter 2

Why Should I Read This? What Good Will It Do?

"Great events turn on small hinges."–

Stephen King The Institute

These questions may be the first in your mind upon opening our book as well as several others you never thought to ask. We aim to address many of these questions. If you picked our book up, you or someone you know may be struggling with health and weight issues and it's time to ask yourself a few questions.

Are you willing to be uncomfortable? Notice I didn't say be in pain, in misery, or sad or depressed. I said **uncomfortable** *(for a short while)* in order to feel better and not be sad, depressed, and in pain? **Discomfort is often mistaken for pain.**

This book is intended for individuals who are interested and willing to challenge themselves in just such a way. Are you open to learning from the real-life experiences of two women who successfully achieved significant weight loss?

We offer insights and guidance for helping others lose between fifteen to one hundred and fifty pounds. We did. Maybe you want to try new ways to feel better or feel more control over your food and eating habits, maybe you want to eat with deliberation rather than compulsion. It's also for anyone who could possibly want to save money on food and medications.

We would like to think it's for anyone who wants to feel understood and not alone in this battle. If in your struggles you need a little non-judgmental relief, we hope this helps you feel seen, heard or understood. Anyone who feels intimidated or inadequate to address these major challenges and to those needing a circle of supportive friends, we hope this offers options. If you're feeling overwhelmed by the changes you need or want to make, perhaps our insights will inspire you, making the challenges seem less daunting.

Our aspiration lies in the methodology MJ, and I adopt for this venture. Maybe you've heard all this before and just needed our particular brand of humor with the subject matter because we also think many people, while working in the health and diet space can take themselves way too seriously! We plan to offer email lists on platforms like Patreon for communication with our readers and followers. We mean it. Contact us with feedback, questions, ideas and let's start a movement between everyone we each connect with. We hope "Each One, Teach One" succeeds and we support each other by any means available.

We are hoping to help you come up with new ideas and coping mechanisms for making tweaks and shifts in your lifestyles. It's always about training and habits yet so few of us know HOW to shift those habits from bad to good. As an overall concept, changing one habit is hard enough so changing habits, *(plural)* can be intimidating.

My big thing, OUR big thing is focusing on changing habits by using incremental time blocks. The human mind is fundamentally geared for change but if you're looking at these changes you want to make in terms of your lifetime, your ability to predict anything in the future can make you anxious. We don't want that. Anxiety is resistance and many of us soothe our anxiety with food.

Even thinking in terms of a week elicits fear of the unknown. The uncertainty sets up anxiety, making us prefer familiar routines *(A.K.A habits)* because we don't exactly know what to do with any given circumstance during the week. What steps do we take from Monday to Sunday? Our fear of losing established systems *(also habits)* and losing this kind of familiarity can be discomforting. For some, familiarity breeds comfort and habits become associated with safety and correctness to such a degree, it takes on a "moral force" in their minds. Breaking habits effectively become immoral and how are we supposed to do that? Don't think so much and so far.

We live our lives in twelve-hour increments because concerning ourselves with each and every habit on a daily basis would get overwhelming if we thought about the long-term. The habits we've successfully re-wired are solidly reset now so we don't worry about them too much. The twelve-hour rule is generally for newer habits we are trying to establish. We also posit replacing bad habits rather than trying to just drop them.

Often a "bad" habit is part of a routine and if you try to drop said habit without putting a better one in its place, you create more anxiety. Try both out and see what works for you. Drop it or replace it.

We know how important sleep is to weight management and your general health, right? It's so important I want to plug in some answers for those who work alternate shifts. While doing shift work, you need to **"shift"** your circadian rhythm to help you stay healthier. Implementing and dogmatically following a few good habits here will improve your sleep.

Use bright light therapy at the start of your shift to signal your body it's time to be awake, and wear super dark shades while avoiding bright light on your way home to help your body wind down. Use blackout curtains and ear plugs or some form of noise cancelling when you sleep. You want your brain to think everyone else is asleep too. If I worked nights again, I would probably soundproof my room like a recording studio.

Keep your sleep and wake times as consistent as possible, even on days off to help stabilize your internal clock. Essentially you should be living like a vampire or a Mogwai. The sun burns and there should be no sun and bright lights. Sun lamps should only be on during the nighttime. Eating your meals at regular times and in sync with your work schedule reinforces the new rhythm.

Are you willing to have an open mind and try new things? Would you be interested in taking a proactive role in your own health status and treatments? Are you tired of blindly following standard medical practices with nothing more than a, "Thank you, Doctor, no I have no questions." While you're hurried out the door.

Would it make you angry if I told you we are fast losing autonomy over our own healthcare and medical treatments? What if I said medical knowledge and decision making is systematically kept from us because 2we don't understand or are incapable of grasping *difficult* medical speak"? Would you be surprised or angered if you thought alternative information was being suppressed based on the idea we are too dumb to know better or because there is money involved? What if this idea could be specifically targeted to anyone of color, race, or lower economic status? Maybe it's nothing so deep and you're just really curious about other weight loss stories.

Well, if this book can get you curious it is for you. We would love for this book to help even one individual interested in getting behind the wheel of their own **health** and their own **care**, *healthcare.*

This book is not about who we are, even though it's entirely who we are and what we've experienced.

WE ARE NOT DOCTORS AND HAVE NO FORMAL TRAINING OR CERTIFICATIONS OF ANY KIND.
We have had SUCCESS and quite a bit of it!

I have spent many hours reading, researching and exploring information from various sources in order to help myself, and now MJ and other friends. The information I've gleaned and utilized to the best of our understanding is from great resources you, yourself can find online. We will share links and references to the experts whose work I have researched over the years.

There are some things people don't want to think about let alone talk about. For example, can you be comfortable with your own poop and pee? Can you look down at it before sending it to its watery grave, because you really should be looking, studying it. It is one of the best ways for us here at home to see what is going on inside our bodies.

Can you get comfortable with your periods and learning more than you ever thought you needed to know about your own menstrual cycles? Women have to. We MUST take our cycles and our hormones into consideration for everything we do, and weight management is no exception. Maybe you're a woman who has struggled with chaotic and grievous cycles for a while now and would like to possibly manage or change it for the better.

For example, did you know fat is its own hormone factory? Not only must we argue with our typical hormone fluctuations, but excess body fat disrupts the balance further, contributing to things like Polycystic Ovarian Syndrome and heavy menstrual flow. For PCOS, intermittent fasting may help manage symptoms and improve menstrual regularity. For general menstrual health, fasting should be approached cautiously and in accord with your cycle since periods of low estrogen like the week before menstruation can further stress your body, particularly with long-term fasting.

Intermittent and long-term fasting are our favorite management tools and both MJ, and I have never had any unfavorable effects from either. We've done all forms of fasting and worked our way incrementally to seventy-two hours every three months or so. Once a year, we will do in excess of five or more with our personal record being fourteen days. To be clear, fasting should be done along with your medical practitioners' guidance and what works for us may not be for you. You can, however, experiment with any new tools you discover as long as you do it safely and with provider's consultation.

If you are willing to go the distance of 187 pages and be okay with your own decision to buy and read without expecting overnight success, then this book is for you. If you understand there is some truth to almost everything you've learned about food and weight loss and that nothing should be taken as dogma or as a one size fits all *(that's just bullshit)* this book is for you.

It's not about being a super-model, a super sports-star, an athlete, or even one who can afford programs, tricks and gadgets. You might want to try new things just for fun, but feel it's impossible.

MJ always wanted to go kayaking. Her large size limited her range of motion and made it hard to reach around her body on a stationary, stable toilet. She struggled to manage her own bathroom needs, never mind getting down to balance a kayak bobbing up and down on a slippery riverbank.

Well, after only five months we had her out there on the Saint John's River in a kayak. Keep in mind the average kayak has a maximum weight capacity of two hundred and fifty to three hundred pounds. By this point she had lost fifty-seven pounds, which is roughly eleven and a half pounds a month.

What exactly she did in those first steps will be discussed in later chapters. If your ADD is kicking in, or you just want to get to it, feel free to jump ahead, jump around.

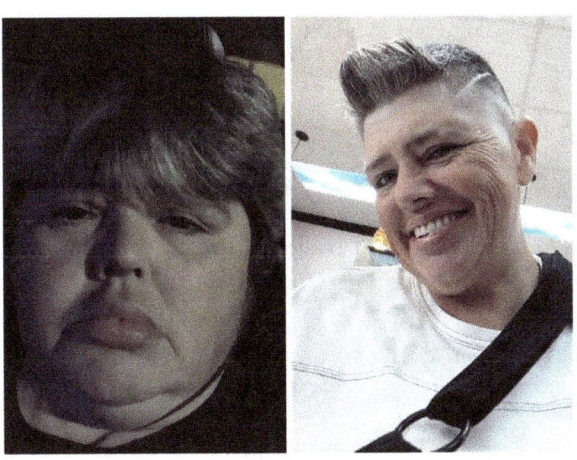

Figure 5: Opposites in the extreme.

A Kayaker's Story

Transcripts Audio Journal

"Every paddle stroke carved away the weight I once carried–on my body, in my mind. The river didn't just lead me forward; it stripped me down to strength."–

MJ Cutsinger

RENEE: So, MJ, let's talk about another interesting experience we just had. It's been what, two years now since the very first time you went kayaking with me and Diana?

MJ: Yeah, that's correct. Go ahead, tell the story.

RENEE: First of all, we were just in the river again, three days ago I think it was?

MJ: We were.

RENEE: I made a comment to you. Do you remember what it was?

MJ: I think it was something like,

"Remember the first time you went with us how you almost didn't fit in the kayak?"

RENEE: Yes, and you remembered being afraid. You said,

"I'll tip over and fall in the water. It's a good thing I know how to swim." When you went out with us for your very first time, the water line was close to spilling over into your kayak because you were so heavy. Now, I noticed how low the water marked a line beneath you in your kayak. You were sitting high and straight up on the surface. Diana even mentioned it.

"MJ, I bet the water line was different huh?" She said to you on Messenger. She brought it to both of our attention.

MJ: Yeah, the whole craft felt different, the maneuverability was a lot smoother.

RENEE: Did you find anything to be easier this time otherwise?

MJ: Keeping up with you because you're fast as hell!

RENEE: Well, I am training you know, to be some hurrah Viking, warrior, longship-rowing princess. Good luck keeping up with me still, I got some powerful shoulders! *(both laughing)*

MJ: Yeah, and you've got a quick, slinky kayak while I've got this big fish boat of a yak.

RENEE: Tell me really, how moving was it for you this second time around?

MJ: I screamed in my head,

"Dude! Check yourself out! You're out here on the same river you were on a year ago to the day." This experience was totally different than the first time. I felt so strong again, like I did when I was young and when nothing could hold me down. Even the landscape looked different that day. It was the same, but different. In that moment I was more connected to myself than I think I have ever been. It was surreal, I felt outside of myself looking in and saying,

"Aha! This is what life is supposed to feel like." I knew THIS is who and what I want to be.

RENEE: Then we were in Fort Myers, and we kayaked all the way out to a little island in the middle of the river remember?

MJ: I had a bit of a struggle keeping up you know. I guess the Caloosahatchee River is quite wide with a strong current. I wasn't down to my goal weight yet, but you know I had come a long way. It wasn't until our second time out to the island I realized how much power I could put behind something like rowing a kayak versus just throwing my bulk around. My size wasn't working for me anymore. It was now about working individual muscle groups I had not used in a long, long time. So, learning to be little, yes, I called myself little, has been quite a challenge.

When we kayaked the other day, you were way ahead of me. I knocked about in this boat which had become too big for me, but two years ago would have been sinking beneath my weight. It's like I'm really learning how to do things and it's quite different.

RENEE: Does it ever feel a bit like loss too, change usually does?

MJ: Any change, even good change?

RENEE: Yeah, I guess it does but, with a sense of loss also comes a new sense of purpose though, right? Because now you know what it's like to work those individual muscle groups. What was it like sitting in the kayak now, versus then?

MJ: I looked over at you and said,

"Look at this!" I was sitting in the kayak cross legged. Back then on our first trip, sitting cross legged was not possible. In fact, sitting cross legged at all wasn't possible.

RENEE: Yeah, I remember the very first time we went kayaking I was worried about you not being able to handle yourself and I kept looking back. I didn't really notice how you were sitting because I was worried about the kayak not being able to keep you above water. You were pretty low.

MJ: Well, I was straight-legged the whole time you know, and my back was killing me. I was feeling aches and pains where I never felt any before in my life.

RENEE: Yet you did it like a champ! What made you paddle through it? You stayed out with us the entire time. I can only imagine kayaking was not your idea of a good time, and you were back there struggling so hard. Diana and I were just paddling away, and it must have been super frustrating for you. I would have felt damn agitated and probably would not have had much fun.

MJ: I wasn't frustrated or agitated. I was exhausted.

RENEE: So, where did you get the motivation to keep paddling?

MJ: Determination and well, I don't like to fail. I don't like to be the brunt of any jokes. I like to come out ahead and that's how I've been getting through this journey. I'm just trying to come out ahead you know, see where I can go with it, see how far I can take it to reach goals and that's what I'm doing.

When we went the other day, I was working on those new muscles and they hurt, but when we came back, I felt like a million bucks! After our run with the Port Saint Lucie River, I felt really good. I felt accomplished.

RENEE: And we saw a baby gator!

MJ: And lots of beautiful birds.

RENEE: A beautiful, big osprey!

MJ: Yes, and I look forward to getting back into the water. I feel my next goal is going to be getting physically fit. I've still got another twenty-five pounds or so I would like to lose. I've pinpointed areas for improvement such as my abdomen, sections of my back, and other regions needing to be toned. This is my new purpose, to get toned and muscular.

RENEE: Indeed. Purpose works together with passion. Your goal now is to be toned and muscular but why is this important to you? The reason why is closer to your purpose. Having a purpose gives added fuel to the fire of passion and makes discipline effortless. Without it, motivational advice and willpower are ineffective. So now you and I must get back into the gym or at least we start adding more muscle challenges like doing our nightly walks with ankle and wrist weights.

MJ: Oh yeah, I see your wheels turning. You're making plans and programs again.

RENEE: Count on it.

End of Transcript

Figure 6: MJ downtown West Palm Beach Christmas Celebration!

Figure 7: MJ hard at work in Oaktown Indiana 2017.

Chapter 3
Typical Obstacles with a Plan for Change

"The chains of habit are too weak to be felt until they are too strong to be broken"–
Samuel Johnson

This time WILL be different! You will see. We will discuss familiar hurdles and common difficulties faced, as well as unique approaches for a different outcome.

Today as always, we are concerned about **money,** right? Some of us are so tight on budget we squeak. It would be lying to say you won't feel a pinch in your wallet or that the budget changes you must make won't seem a little daunting at first, but it will work. You can succeed. Your new habits and lifestyle changes will aid in your ability to afford better quality food.

Organic, whole foods without pesticides, hormones, antibiotics and genetically modified organisms are significantly more expensive and getting more so every day. These groceries can be hard to find due to your location and supply chain issues. When availability issues arise, so does the cost.

Even if you aren't shopping for organics, just buying fresh produce or fresh anything costs more money than it does to buy a case of macaroni and cheese. It is more cost prohibitive to buy the items for a good salad than it is to buy a "burger" from your favorite fast-food chain. Whenever we leave any store now, even popular and supposedly cheaper ones, we notice a two-hundred-dollar grocery bill requires a lot more bags to carry when full of processed, preservative laden stuff like ramen, mac n cheese, and microwave meals for .99 cents.

Two hundred dollars brings back only a few bags to carry when filled with fresh meats, dairy, or produce. The moral of the story—we must find ways to absorb this higher expense for good, clean, non-toxic food because if we don't, we'll pay for our health in other less enjoyable ways. It may be at your doctors with medicines and co-pays, or your insurance premiums because your lab work scared your carrier. Maybe you miss time at work because you get sick a lot. The same goes for our kids. When they get sick and miss school, who stays home with them?

The bags filled with fresh goods are fewer and lighter and don't stretch as far. On top of more expense per serving for organic or fresh food, the average person has no idea what a true "portion" is. A true portion is typically a handful. When you pour yourself a bowl of cereal, hopefully something like nut and granola clusters with no added sugar, the bowl is usually several servings.

Next time, stick your hand in and only eat what you can hold in your fist. The idea here is to train yourself to eat considerably less. Less food per serving equals less per meal, less per day, per week, and per month equaling a lower grocery bill regardless of what you paid two hundred dollars for. We trained ourselves to eat a lot less, so it evens out.

When you eat fresh, whole food, your body receives more nutrients and becomes satiated more easily, which can also lead to eating less over time. As you grow and train through your journey, your desire for things will shrink and so will the burden on your wallet. Don't forget to shop around and use discount points and coupons. Get better at shopping with savings by doing more research if you have to.

I often thought about trying to put together a grocery shop co-op situation with friends and/or neighbors. You know, like a food club! A food club where members collaboratively create weekly menus, share cooking and shopping duties, and split grocery costs. Shopping online can offer better deals or provide various alternative options and let's not forget all of these great meal plan and delivery services now.

Availability

Organic whole foods are often difficult to acquire based on your location, shortages and supply chain issues. Here is another gift from the internet age. What we are not close to, we can have delivered to us very quickly and usually cost effectively.

I do suggest doing your best to buy locally first, you'd be amazed at how many small farms or farmer's markets are hidden away in your area. If growing it yourself or sourcing from a local farm or market is not feasible or affordable, consider looking online.

I also wonder why we don't start a garden co-op with our neighborhood. Why can't Jim next door grow tomatoes on the side of his house, and we grow cucumbers? Lisa down the street has more space for lettuce to grow because the person who lived there before left a big sand box she can put up on blocks for a raised garden bed.

Here in my county, even though I live on the edge of downtown in a major city, I'm allowed to have five chickens as pets. Five will produce a dozen eggs a week which is enough to barter and trade for Jim's tomatoes. Why not right? Don't be afraid of the learning curve. It can be great fun to try.

Hit up friends and family who live elsewhere and who may have access to good deals and hard to find items. Form social groups, either in real life or on internet platforms. Granted, becoming backyard farmers or starting our own neighborhood co-op and barter system is a bit ambitious and chicken husbandry is realistic for only a handful of us, but you track what I'm saying. FIND A WAY TO EAT BETTER. We can all do this together.

Family and Friends

I know it sounds a little wrong to include family and friends in the section dedicated to problems because aren't they supposed to be part of our support system? Yes, they should be and most often are when they learn just how serious you are.

Remember though, they are people too, with their own agendas. We all operate from the place of our own hopes, fears and flaws with at least a few poor coping mechanisms to share with you. They have good ones too as long as you're aware of the bad ones and can weed through them all.

Keep in mind they have their own perspective on you as well. They may have witnessed you trying health and diet routines before. Perhaps they don't realize the strength of your commitment this time and are in the "humoring you" frame of mind without either of you realizing it. The interventions of family and friends can often get in the way.

Usually, they are well meaning with their comments, advice, stories and awkward feelings or opinions about your journey but, it can be confusing and conflicting. Pick your course of action and stick to it! Listen to everyone else giving different bits of advice with the mute button on. Read their closed captions but leave them on mute for a while. Trying new things can sometimes provoke fearful reactions, especially if they are somewhat controversial, even as you seem to become healthier and happier.

For the most part, these are projections of their own thoughts and feelings, but they are well-meaning and interested which is a good thing. You can entertain a few people, listen to them sincerely, take away useful insights, and dismiss the rest respectfully.

There are those who aren't so well meaning and are intent on sabotaging your success for many reasons. People often don't realize they are doing it. It can be a subconscious thing for them as well so don't sacrifice your energy to anger, it's too distracting. It can also be stress inducing which will cause a cortisol flood in your bloodstream.

Avoiding cortisol floods to the best of your ability is paramount to a healthy lifestyle. Cortisol is a body's natural stress response to anything requiring urgent care or attention. So, start saving your care and attention and truly limit what gets labeled URGENT.

Sometimes the saboteurs look like friends and sometimes they are friends who sabotage us without knowing it. Family can do the same. Sometimes our friends and family will fight you the hardest and it will surprise and even hurt you.

Why would they be like this you might ask, well, this my friends is a whole book by itself. What I will say is you can treat the saboteurs and friends the same. No matter how well meaning anyone is, at the end of the day, you have to do what feels right for you. You know best the things you have tried and what works and didn't work for you to this point. Don't let other people's fear of change and trying new things get in your way.

I sometimes struggle with my thoughts, which can be challenging. Consequently, I tend to approach interactions with others in a similar manner, regardless of their intentions. I invite them to a table for two in some pleasant little café in my head, or to my own kitchen table.

I serve them a cup of green tea, unsweetened of course, with a few berries and honey while I give them a set amount of time to express themselves. I take notes sometimes because even those who try to detract from us may have good advice or things to teach us.

Also, when people see you taking notes, they feel valued and heard, and sometimes that's all they were after in the first place. Humor people, but maintain YOUR perspective and when the tea and honey are gone you get up from the table *(real or imagined)* and show them the door. Leave them to their own and go in peace. Smile and wave at them. When all else fails, just smile and wave.

Anxiety and depression

Throughout my life as well as MJ in hers, we share a lot of deep-rooted traumas. The reactions and triggers we have developed over the years continue to take education, awareness, and reprogramming to stop them from derailing our progress.

I spent mandatory time on a psych ward when I was younger because I struggled with depression so deep, I was a suicide risk. Two things stand out as far as what helped me get out of my downward spiral. Journaling and attending many group therapy sessions as well as

42

private ones too in which I frequently shared what I wrote. Journaling and sharing made my therapy even more productive.

As I write, I ponder what has been the most effective solution for managing anxiety and depression in my life. I remember my therapist on the ward giving me an assignment. He said I should write about it in my journal and then go find something outside of myself to do for another person. He said,

"Go help a life or save a life." So dark was my head space, I could not fathom that this man had his own head anywhere else other than up his own ass.

As it turns out, he was right and has been right several times along the course of my life. The day after he gave this advice, I went to the room of an old man who had been placed on the ward with us. He was there because he talked of nothing but dying. He was eighty-something with contagious skin disorders and was deprived of human touch. He was blind and had one living relative he hadn't seen in a long time. Yeah, he was ready to check out.

I was told he loved to read, but he couldn't anymore because of his eyes. So, I took a Reader's Digest book from the day room shelves and spent every spare moment I had in "Club Head" sitting by his bedside and reading stories to him. His name was Eugene, and his favorite story was about Thor the bear. He would smile when he heard my voice and ask the nurses for me on the few occasions I didn't show.

He told his last relative, his niece, all about me on the phone and told her I had become the light of his day. She made a special trip to come and thank me, and he gave me purpose outside of myself. The universe can be odd. It turns out I knew his niece, she was the only girl in high school who made me feel safe and liked.

Fast forward a decade. My second divorce was speeding towards me, my second house was in foreclosure and things just seemed to be falling apart all around me yet again, for the third decade in a row. I never again approached Baker-acting levels of depression but, I was close.

I remembered my counselor and his advice to "change a life, save a life" so I went to the county animal shelter, a kill shelter, and I asked them to show me the cats on death row who were going to die if they weren't adopted that night. A beleaguered vet-tech led me down a hall lined with stacked cages to stand in front of an ugly door labeled 'Euthanasia'. He explained how they started with the stack closest to the scratched and dented door, so I asked for the one on top.

The first cage to go housed an entire litter of kittens. I was told they were feral, and they wouldn't be a good pet, so I picked one out anyway with the help of my son. My cat lived with me in pampered bliss almost to this day. His name is Harles J. He was an old man when he passed on the twenty-third of September, right before we finished this manuscript. He continues to be a source of joy and a reminder of the difference I can make in this world that frequently feels pointless and overwhelming.

Living outside of myself has been my main coping strategy for mental health issues, including grief from loss. Journaling about it all is number two. Have I said journaling enough yet?

Journaling about how, what, where and when can work wonders for you. Not only can you go back and look for patterns (habits) or cause

44

and effect, but when you read it out loud to yourself, you're talking things through. When you hear your own voice reflecting back, you can often answer your own questions or give yourself long-awaited solutions to problems you didn't know you had. Understanding your triggers and habits is crucial for adopting a holistic approach to life.

When MJ first started this journey, she didn't tell anyone. Instead, she began making journal entries about her progress and how it made her feel. She never mentioned her eating and lifestyle plan either. She just did it and let them watch and ask questions. Frequently your friends will get inspired once they realize the strength of your desire and start following you with the same force and dedication. Now, you are part of the movement– congratulations!

Pharmaceuticals

Before we go any further on the topic of pharmaceuticals, let it be known I was not a fan. I personally took every measure possible to avoid prescription medications. I did my level best with ice packs, heating pads, water therapy, aromatherapy, massage, meditation, and sleep to avoid even taking Tylenol. I do take a lot of vitamins and supplements to help me deal with my health issues but, it is a never-ending task of learning and exploration as well as laborious in research and follow-through.

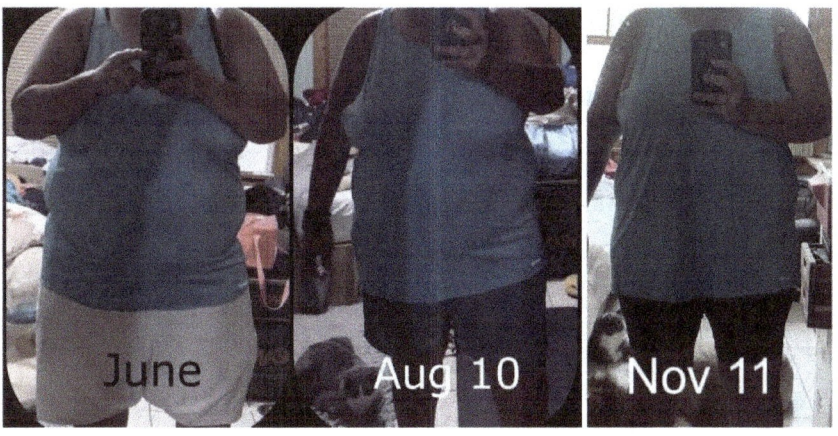

Figure 8: MJ's progress in five short months.

Figure 9: MJ hamming it up in front of the camera. One-year difference.

I can't. I am not your doctor; I'm not any kind of doctor. I do, however, strongly believe lifestyle changes can lead to health improvements and reduce the need for medications. In the meantime, as you begin to experience better health you will do your own research, take notes, and question everything!

Obviously, the pharmaceuticals we take for pain, injury, depression, anxiety and so much more, all play a part in weight gain or loss. Some of these medicines could become unnecessary for you in the future. Eliminating or reducing the number of medications you take can even be part of your goal. I don't think it comes as a surprise by saying our medicines are over prescribed and are the first answer to everything. MJ and I have running jokes about the pharmaceutical ads on TV.

"Do you wake up in the morning and fart when you eat beans? Do you blink when you sneeze or cough? If so, you may have Tardismisconceptual predispositional eye rolling disease and our drug can make it stop. So, what if your teeth fall out and you get a particularly nasty case of anal mold, you can stop rolling your eyes or itching your butt." Obviously, this is a fake commercial I made up and an exaggeration of commercial scripts *(not by much)*, but you get the point.

There is a drug for everything. (2)Thanks to the 21st Century Cures Act in 2016 which lowered the bar by requiring even less reliable data and frequently no controlled clinical trials, it's become the wild west of prescription living. I am now a diabetic. I have a continuous glucose monitor on my person and I find it to be very helpful as it tells me exactly what my blood sugar is at all times. I am using this to help me adjust my eating habits in a herculean effort to avoid taking Metformin or insulin.

I read a book written by an actual doctor who has authored multiple works on the subject. He was on the faculty of Harvard Medical School for twenty-five years teaching healthcare policy, he was a family physician for twenty-two years, and an unpaid consultant to the FBI and DOJ. His accolades go on and he obviously knows what he's talking about.

(3)In his book, he notes manufacturers have convinced doctors to prescribe over twenty billion dollars of insulin yearly for type two diabetes. Giving us a direct indication of marketing's strong influence over scientific evidence in prescribing decisions.

This is a book everyone should read! I'm not kidding. Read it! **John Abramson, MD, MSc "Sickening – How Big Pharma Broke American Health Care."**

Now I know this might have been less than entertaining and very sciency. It may have given you PTSD from school days but, it's super important because when you read his book, you are going to understand how many ways we are being fooled and manipulated for others' financial gains.

The stale and predictable arguments, "Trust the science" or "Science is real" have become cliché and while science IS real, so is greed, corruption and marketing. Biased statistics, incomplete studies, and pharmaceutical marketing standards impact our safety, health, and well-being. You may be asking yourself, are marketing agencies affecting my doctor's treatment of me, really? Yes, REALLY. Question everyone regardless of the initials by their name. After reading Doctor

Abramson's book, one might question whether or not pharmaceutical companies persuaded doctors to lower the diagnostic threshold for diabetes in order to label everyone as diabetic. It certainly generates more revenue.

Pharmaceutical companies have a history of this type of malfeasance, with all or some of their drugs. They sponsor studies and then redact the findings in their reports or don't account for them at all. When results come, they only report the ones showing favorable outcomes for their product or at the very least, they're heavily weighted.

Making matters worse, [4]another study found doctors being encouraged to prescribe certain medications with financial incentives. Intentional? Maybe. Directly or indirectly, who can really say but, the net results are the same. Again, read this doctor's book in his own words to be sure we are not making this up or making wild accusations. It's an incredibly enlightening read in which many conflicts of interest are illustrated. We expect you will read the whole thing for yourself.

In our opinion, modern medicine has its place and saves lives. It is, however, corrupted by big industry and conflicts of interest at every turn. We must do our own homework now and get our hands on as much information as possible. There is much more to say about pharmaceuticals in general. I selected diabetes as a focal point due to its close association with weight management concerns.

We take many medications because we simply can't do without them and they will have multiple side effects, derailing weight loss and other negative impacts on our lives. "Proven science" is not always what gets published, and I am certain many side-effects unreported or unforeseen are yet to come, including weight management issues.

However, we should strive to keep our attention on the things **we can change**. We can each become intimately aware of every message and feeling our body gives us and we can stop outsourcing our own self-care to any medical professional with a piece of paper stating they know better. We can speak amongst ourselves and find ways to compensate or adjust our habits no matter how hard the necessary discipline may seem.

I'm not saying don't listen to your doctors but don't listen to them exclusively of everything else including your own body and instincts. Do your own research and ask questions even if it makes everyone uncomfortable. Don't be afraid to investigate what you are told, what you take, and what you eat. Don't be afraid to ask them to try alternative methods first. Your doctors and other professionals should be willing to collaborate with you as a team on your body, if not, find a new doctor who will.

One day you could be free of or have a lot less medications and until then, we can practice new dialogues with our doctors. We can do our best to mitigate our own problems rather than continuing a one size fits all approach to everything including our pharmaceuticals.

I would urge everyone to research how most medications released for use by the public, do not get their own studies for their effects on women specifically. So, most women are taking drugs designed and measured in doses fit for men. As women, we do not have the same reactions to these drugs per dose.

Consider statins: [5]Dr. Abramson's book highlights the case of a female patient, exemplifying women's inequality in healthcare and medical research. With no prior history of heart disease or strokes, she was prescribed a statin based on guidelines from the National Cholesterol Education Program and the National Heart, Lung, and Blood Institute. Her cholesterol level indicated a slightly higher risk of heart disease. This assessment was conducted using guidelines from 2001, which significantly increased the number of individuals prescribed statins compared to the 1993 guidelines. Most of these individuals were healthy except for certain "risk factors."

Now, according to some doctors in the Journal of American Medical Association who published an [6]"executive summary" twelve pages long *(a summary should not be twelve pages)* women without any previous heart disease would experience "positive effects" from statins.

[7]Meanwhile, clinical trials of statins showed contradictory results amongst the general population that weren't included in the full-length report and there have been no clinical trials which have shown statins to be effective for women.

[8]It has been asserted that recommending statin therapy for women of "low risk" is solely based on the documented benefits of statins for men with similar risk factors and experts admitted to insufficient studies on women period. In short, **statins' effects on women are unknown,** and assumptions were made based on results for men. Being so invested in our own health care, we should regularly evaluate its effectiveness. We continually check if our current treatments are achieving their goals and assess any side effects causing additional problems beyond the original issues.

When you ask yourself these kinds of questions, you should prepare to change your dialogue with doctors and give yourself more choices in how YOUR body gets treated. Ask them if what they are prescribing can be substituted by a change in lifestyle, a smaller dosage or less active drugs.

Your doctors will likely give you push back on a lot of what we are doing here so find doctors who believe your health is a team effort and who take a more holistic and whole-body approach to health care. They may be hard to find but they are out there, and their ranks are growing.

Social Life

We all know our social life intrudes upon our goals. Whether it's a desire to drink less, drink socially, quit smoking, or indulge less in poor eating choices. Hanging out with our friends and coworkers can be problematic. When you're not going out with your friends to smoke, drink and eat what are you doing for a social life?

You can address these issues ahead of time. Start by being the one who initiates plans and comes up with alternatives to get the group moving or doing actively fun things. Everybody goes bowling or to escape rooms, sporting events and shows. Facilitate activities with your peeps that keep you all focused on things other than eating and drinking. If all else fails and you simply can't avoid a drinking situation without a glass in hand, there are several options.

There are nonalcoholic versions of everything. If you pull your server or your bartender aside and tell them to give you a mock-tail cocktail in the glass its alcoholic cousin is usually served in, no one's going to know the difference. These are all things I have successfully tried and enjoyed.

I spoke to a manager at Rocco's Tacos because they put my mock-tail in a regular beverage glass instead of the margarita glass. He graciously re-poured the drink in a standard margarita glass, ensuring my business partners at the meeting remained unaware. There are always alternatives!

You can also feel a slight buzz and relaxation from fermented drinks like Kombucha and fruit flavored vinegar. Flavored vinegar made by Kosterina and available on Amazon sounds weird, but it is very tasty and satisfying when mixed with club soda. Fermented beverages are also great for your gut and immune system.

When I feel like I must have an alcohol buzz or "take the edge off" I try and choose the lowest sugar option available. Options include but are not limited to: Bacardi 00 with a diet soda, Bloody Mary mixed with V8 juice to avoid added carbs from bar mixes and Prosecco with Saint Germain make a nice cocktail. Michelob Ultra is a decent beer and the list goes on. These are not zero carb or zero sugar options however, so if drinking is unavoidable stop at one or two of these.

After picking one or two of these alternatives, you can nurse your drink for hours. You gotta kind of make out with your glass and hold it, caress it, stare deeply into its enchanting movements as you twirl it about. Why? It gives you a way to mix and mingle with your cohorts and avoid questions if you want to. It's less pressure and you'll drink less while you stand there looking like you don't have a care in the world. You'll appreciate it for its beauty in color, taste, and aroma, not just its alcohol content.

Saint Germaine has a floral aroma with citrus and sweet notes from the elderflower plant. The colors of the alcohol, whether it's the rich Amber of whiskey, the crystal clarity of vodka, or the deep red of an Australian Shiraz wine become more vibrant and inviting. As your glass is tilted or rotated, the light passing through is bent and distorted, casting a warm glow around the edges of the liquid. It catches the tiny imperfections in the glass, creating an illusion of depth and making it appear multi-dimensional.

Notice how your drink mingles with the light, sparkling, and adding allure to your drink. This interplay between light, glass, and liquid is both elegant and captivating, making the simple act of enjoying a drink a sensory delight.

(The authors of this book are not spokesmodels or brand ambassadors and are not being compensated for their time or opinions.)
Don't think taboo, think FOR YOU! Embrace don't chase!

Give love and thought to the food and beverages you sustain your body with. Most people live by the idea of avoidance as if "out of sight" really is "out of mind." We suggest doing the opposite. Think about it all the time but think about it all with love. I'm telling you to develop a romantic relationship with all of it. Give your food and drink so much attention as you would a lover, with deep understanding, a lot of respect and a little give and take.

These descriptive paragraphs may seem to be nothing more than poetry at first but, I am attempting to demonstrate growing passions and an almost feral attachment to your mouth. Animals use all of their senses when hunting their food because they eat to live, they don't live to eat.

Wild animals also often rely on their groups for protection and help. Why should we feel bad when we can't tackle challenges alone or don't want to face our problems in isolation? We're so focused on a "self" culture and on the power and responsibility of the individual, we forgot it can be OK to look for safety and success in numbers rather than succeeding at everything all the time on our own.

In a can-do world, it's hard to accept not all of us are built the same way. Some of us NEED a village and to have our hands held the whole way. This is acceptable too as a lack of cohesive effort often hinders the progress of many individuals. We have got to let ourselves fail sometimes without turning into a self-hater and without berating ourselves with words like failure. Do not keep reminding yourself you screwed up by programming the failure word into your mind. Admit it once, you check and correct yourself and move on.

Mindless Munchies

This is what we call it when we indulge in emotional or habitual eating for comfort, such as decompressing at night in front of the tv or in bed. Whenever I have my beloved movie night or I'm binge-watching shows on Netflix, particularly under the influence of THC, I really struggle. There are a few things we have found to appease our inner snack beast. We have experimented with a lot of cold, raw veggies such as sugar snap peas, snow peas, or even fresh green beans dipped in Marie's Blue Cheese Dressing *(one of the few with almost no sugar)*. We're looking for a "popcorn feel."

For example, I love steamed and salted Edamame while watching a movie because the smell, texture and salt are very reminiscent of popcorn with the same repetitive hand-to-mouth action. It even starts tasting like popcorn to me. THC's appetite stimulation is more about pleasure and reward stimulus due to an increased sensitivity to food aromas and flavors, making sugary or fatty foods more appealing.

At the same time, salt cravings can stem from dehydration or sodium imbalance. So I found I could appease my reward seeking, ghrelin producing, endocannabinoid flooded system with the strong flavors of fat and salt rather than sugary carbs. Don't forget your thirty-two ounces of water too so you're not confused by signals of dehydration. There is of course concerns about salt intake as well, so we frequently balance salty snacks with potassium supplements.

Pork rinds are good too for a "mouth feel." I like peeling, halving, and scooping a cucumber to fill with cream cheese and Everything Bagel seasoning. I can fool myself into thinking I'm eating a bagel. Every day I see a new keto friendly snack on the market.

For the soda feeling, I was using sparkling, flavored water or my vinegars with club soda but, I realized the carbonation was contributing to my heartburn. I also learned any beverage with carbonation saps your body of magnesium to process the gasses, so we take magnesium supplements.

Again, diet drinks mess with your taste receptors as much as regularly sweetened products. Some animal studies suggest certain artificial sweeteners might trigger insulin spikes or affect insulin sensitivity. So why mess around to find out? There are always other options, you need only look. Now we have chat and AI to help us.

Pain and Injury

The next big issue on my personal list is pain and injury. I have been living with relapsing and remitting Multiple Sclerosis since I was first diagnosed at age twenty-one. Over the decades, I have managed both good days at the gym and days when I am unable to get out of bed and need to move cautiously around my home. In between these extremes, I continue to adjust my habits and routines to maintain my health and activity level. During those in-between days, I have worked with three main concepts to "Get it done."

MJ taught me about using the power of making new memories to bury old ones. It can be a strong motivator and very compelling. Utilizing the adrenaline rage, and pain provides can take you a long way towards accomplishing ones goal or to create impetus and desire. When we combine these with patience and learn to breathe our way through small increments of pain, we build our tolerance to it. We realize pain and injury can seem insurmountable and although we have both experienced similar situations, it is important to recognize that each individual has their own unique tolerance threshold.

Its ok if your journey takes more time, additional months for healing and coping or different tactics altogether. This is super OKAY! Just DON'T QUIT OR GIVE UP. With alternative, flexible and creative ideas, help from doctors, and physical therapists, you can get through it. For MJ, it was a matter of sheer guts and determination. She coped with the pain for a short time during her first, fateful walk on the beach. She pushed through the pain briefly each day in order to have a better, less pain filled life later on.

Figure 10: MJ conversing with Garden Gnomes in Port St. Lucie Florida.

The Walk

Transcripts Audio Journal

"Do not follow where the path may lead.

Go instead where there is no path and leave a trail."– Ralph Waldo Emerson

MJ: Let me start by saying the first walk towards recovery was by far the hardest walk I have ever done for myself. It wasn't only physically challenging, but it was also mentally and emotionally difficult. I drove myself to the beach right before sunrise. After I had my coffee and had Go-Go juice *(water mixed with Apple Cider Vinegar, salt and Crème of Tartar to replace electrolytes)* in tow, I parked at Andy Romano Park; it's a place where I have a lot of history.

This part of the beach once was a magical place for me. Half a mile north of the beach's access point there is a pylon pole alerting beach goers to a shipwreck in the water. Sometimes it's deeply submerged, but frequently you can walk to it on a sandbar.

My mother and I walked to this pole in June of 2017 and as the tide washed out, a starfish was left behind in a pool formed beneath our feet. It was an enchanted moment and a last, cherished memory with my mother who passed away a week later on my birthday. Seven days after mom passed, I was getting married by this pole to the mother of my twins.

In March of 2020 I had an accident while walking my Saint Bernard puppy. I fell and broke my right ankle. It was a trying time in my life as it required surgery and plenty of recovery time. My routine changed from spending time outdoors walking with her or visiting parks and beaches to a more sedentary lifestyle. I got through it but, after a summer of boredom I found myself in the same situation again in October of the same year.

This time my injury was much more severe. I was out with my pup at the baseball diamond where I could let her play off leash. As I closed the gate to secure the perimeter and turned to walk back to her, I somehow managed to walk over the top of my left foot and fell, resulting in yet another scary, compound fracture.

RENEE: For those unfamiliar with the term, a compound fracture is characterized by the broken bone piercing the flesh and tearing through all of your tendons and surrounding tissue.

MJ: Yeah, my bone was sticking out and my foot was practically severed. It was hanging on by an inch and a half of skin and some tendons. We were certain I was going to lose my foot. The surgeon managed to reattach it with the help of plates, screws, and some wires. The recovery was even worse than when I broke the right ankle, and it took longer to heal. Not only was I dealing with the healing process of the left ankle, but the right ankle developed Osteomyelitis.

RENEE: That's a bone infection.

MJ: Yeah, and this resulted in another surgery to remove all the hardware as well as a series of intravenous, antibiotic, therapy treatments daily for a month. Keep in mind I was three hundred forty-seven pounds and could not bear any weight at all. Getting around was super difficult. Getting to and from the hospital for treatment in the middle of winter in southern Indiana took a little grace from a higher power.

I managed to get through the healing process with both feet still attached to my legs and as healthy as they could be considering all they had been through. My marriage was tanking, and choices had to be made. I was in a horribly dark place when I sold my house and relocated to Florida with my sister. Our house was a quick ride to the beach, and I enjoyed driving to it so I could watch the sunrise over the water. It kept me somewhat sane. This new routine gave me something to get up for and a place to go and stare off across the water at this pole.

I can't put into words how much I wanted to walk out to my pole; what it meant to me. I stood on the beach looking at the outline of it and talked myself out of trying so many times. I was sure I couldn't do it, and I almost succumbed to my inner demons and aborted the mission as a lost cause. I guess the day finally came, when after staring at it and longing for it for so many weeks, I just said fuck it. I put one foot in front of the other. I kept my eyes focused on the pole which was a first for me in a long time. I had gotten in the habit of always looking down at my feet to watch them.

This time I couldn't watch my feet; they hurt so fucking bad. I kept my eyes on that damned pole the whole time. This was my pole damn it! I had a beautiful moment with my mom here and my ex would not be my last memory of it. I was all up in my head, feeling worthless, pointless, ashamed I let myself get this way. I think the rage and pain actually pushed me till the pain in my feet became a welcome relief from the turmoil and pain inside. I looked up–

RENEE: And you were there.

MJ: I was there yes. I managed to make it to my pole. I stood there hugging it with every hurting piece of my body and heart, sobbing like a toddler. In my mind it hugged me back, holding onto me and offering comfort in a way I hadn't been able to feel for quite some time. It was a painful experience physically, but more so emotionally. Never did I ever think I would be able to accomplish such a goal, but I did! From that day forward, it became easier, and I became more focused.

Each passing day I became stronger until I managed to build myself up from half a mile to six miles a day. On certain days I felt stronger than others and managed to squeeze out eight miles. Some days I didn't feel strong at all and only managed a mile or two, but I had to try. I didn't want to lose any forward motion. In total, according to the app on my phone, I ended up walking or sometimes hobbling and limping 765.53 miles to and from my pole. Between walking and talking to you and making the other small changes to my life and diet, the weight started sliding off like butter.

RENEE: I remember getting so mad at you for taking such a walk without telling me you were, and I found out about it at the same time I found out the extent of the injuries to your ankles. I was so mad. If I had known the level of injury, I would not have been so pushy about walking, especially in soft sand.

MJ: The soft sand was actually helpful. Close to the water it had just enough give to cushion my ankle from my weight, but it was firm enough to not let my ankles roll.

RENEE: I was also super proud. I still am today and even now as we discuss it, I am blown away by your determination and your fortitude. You are amazing.

So, I hope everyone out there hears her. Even with traumatic injury, pain and physically limiting conditions, there is much to be said about making small changes to improve our situation, even tiny ones in times it seems all hope is lost.

MJ came to Florida to end it all. Instead she was reborn. Encouraged by the mental and emotional benefits of her improved diet and lifestyle, she took her first steps. With superhuman effort, a whole lot of personal fortitude and a bit of strength, she took a life altering and a lifesaving walk.

As we are recording and transcribing this, I am struggling with my own pain. I regretfully realize I may have conquered my last full day of theme park entertainment. I am making strides to heal my daily pain and discomfort, but this type of activity sets me back to deep, too far, and for too long.

I want to respect what my body is telling me and this time it was too much. They say you shouldn't ride these things with certain conditions, and they mean it. I'm super grateful for the experiences and I'm glad MJ and I could do it together. I would do it again because watching MJ's joy was worth every second of the ensuing pain. I also would never advocate doing anything not safe for your personal situation or conditions. Respect and listen to your body at all times.

I guess in the end, what I'm trying to say is find a balance between your physical limitations and your physical "limitations." Respect your situation, listen to your body's signals but, don't be afraid to work with yourself and safely stretch your mind, body, and spirit in order to keep or grow the abilities you still have.

This may not be amusement parks or anything crazy, but you also don't necessarily have to submit to a continued loss of abilities either. Try. Try to keep moving and try to keep reaching physical and emotional goals.

MJ: Thanks to some diet and lifestyle changes, we're able to heal ourselves enough to get enjoyment out of life. It's not over until you're gone.

RENEE: I was telling my dad today, you know, because he's fighting through cancer and after the removal of his esophagus, he can't eat and is wasting away. I was like listen, you know if you follow some basic guidelines for eating, you can fix this and you can do better for your body's current situation. While you may not be able to heal yourself one hundred percent, isn't seventy-five percent better than five?

MJ: Exactly.

RENEE: So, we do what we can for the body we have and its constraints. When you do the best you can for the body you have today, you are rewarding the body you have tomorrow, and so on.

MJ: You feel better.

RENEE: You feel better, and you can make changes and perhaps lessen your limitations and exponentially improve your body's capabilities as they are.

MJ: This is not just about your physical body; it's about improving everything.

RENEE: Which of course, includes your mind.

MJ: The mind...

RENEE: You can't do it without the mind.

MJ: You've got to win the mind game because if you fall out of touch with your own mind game; like tonight when you asked me what made me break my stride–

RENEE: Oh, when we were walking?

MJ: Yes. I had to really put my mind to overcoming my pain and soreness.

RENEE: I think I felt your distress, and I started using my old military cadences to keep you in step with me. I heard you fall back, and I asked you what's wrong.

MJ: Pain, and you wanna know what's funny? You would think after our three-mile jaunt, I would be okay with a shorter walk.

RENEE: Well, as we've said, this doesn't make your arthritis go away.

MJ: No, it doesn't but, I had to remind myself and dig deep through the soreness. I had to stop telling myself it hurt too much because I just did a big walk. These after dinner walks are too important to me.

RENEE: You're just pushing through the pain sometimes.

MJ: Yeah, when we go to Orlando, we don't always follow our own rules including eating habits.

RENEE: Right.

MJ: But, in our defense, we had the kids with us the last few times which makes it harder you know.

RENEE: Yeah right.

MJ: They don't graze on salads like we do.

RENEE: So I may have to spend my time watching all the productions and amazing shows I've never taken the time for now. I was too busy trying to get on rides, but we will continue our yearly sojourns to universal in celebration of my birthday. Otherwise, known as my return to birth or welcome to Earth Day.

MJ: Welcome to earth day!

RENEE: That's right, from now on birthdays are no longer about aging and how long you've been here. It's about once again we welcome you to planet Earth.

End of Transcript

Figure 11: MJ on her way to her new home in Florida 2021 and then MJ returning from her first out of the country travel to Peru in 2024. Such a stark difference in her mind, body, and soul.

Figure 12: Renee and MJ living life to the fullest at Machu Picchu!

Chapter 4
The Secret Recipe, a Key to Success

"Where you tend a rose, my lad a thistle cannot grow."–
The Secret Garden by Frances Hodgins Burnett

We are creatures of habit, bad ones, marginal ones, and good ones. Shifting the balance of our habits is essential for attaining goals. It's been proven we are most successful at the things we do without thinking. We form these habits best by actively "doing" our routines every day. Your chances of success go up almost fifteen percent each day you participate in your own routine. Multiply fifteen percent daily by seven days a week and you've got more than a one hundred percent chance of success, just by making minor changes in your weekly and daily habits.

As I've mentioned, we are very resistant to change. As you read this, your grey matter is telling you,

"I don't like this, it's not gonna work. I don't have time for this." Don't listen, don't even think right now. Just do it, keep reading, argue with yourself later.

Tell your brain you appreciate the insights but, you want to try anyway. Give yourself a chance and THINK about it some other day while you DO it today.

Pecan Pie Please...

TRANSCRIPTS AUDIO JOURNAL

"Stressed spelled backward is desserts. Coincidence? I think not." – Anonymous

MJ: Today, I'm at the point where I know losing a pound here or five pounds there actually makes a difference. It gets me lined up facing the goal posts and just as every five yards gained is closer to scoring a touchdown, each pound lost contributes to my forward drive into the endzone by providing measurable outcomes. Getting momentum, that's something I wanna talk about.

RENEE: Let's talk about it. Tell me how you remember the beginning.

MJ: You said we'd replace some items in my diet with equally satisfying alternatives to add variety, not eliminate them.

Here we are two years later and some of the things you had me put away for a while are coming back into my life now. You know I'm a Funyuns baby. I've had a lot of Funyuns lately but, my metabolism has learned to offset more of my dietary indiscretions it seems. I only fluctuate about ten pounds more or less.

69

Occasionally, I eat onion rings or a chili dog with a beer, but then I resume my routine and after a few days, my weight goes back down. My metabolism is stabilizing as I drop the fat and exchange it for muscle.

RENEE: Yep, this happens! Your hormones and metabolism adjust based on the amount of fat you carry or lose. I don't think it's commonly known, but our fat produces its own hormones and influences your metabolic processes.

Tell me, are you having a tough time right now? Because we've been under more stress for the past six months than either one of us has known in a while. The continuous, intense nature of the stress and round-the-clock care for my father with no relief has rendered me incapable of functioning effectively in other aspects of life.

MJ: Umm… I do know I have completely fallen off my wagon.

RENEE: Me too which is why I asked, and I've gained weight again. I'm currently back to where I was two and a half years ago before you and I met. These same fifteen to twenty-five pounds originally kept me from my goal posts and out of the end zone for so long, I would've tried anything. I started practicing intermittent fasting two years before meeting you.

I started by eating every sixteen hours and would only eat within the remaining eight-hour window. If I ate dinner at six in the evening, I would not eat ANYTHING again and breakfast didn't happen until sixteen hours later at ten in the morning.

At first this was difficult, and I had to rely heavily on my coffee as an appetite suppressant to get me through my typical breakfast time. It got increasingly easier to do until I started going one and then two hours later, frequently without even realizing it. Soon I wouldn't break my fast until noon or one o'clock. My intermittent fasting window had gone from eating every sixteen hours to every eighteen hours and I barely noticed.

It was at this point I began intentionally stretching the time for a challenge. I was getting close to eating only once every twenty-four hours and really questioning my desire to eat every time I felt an urge. Am I actually hungry I thought, or am I feeling apprehensive because I haven't eaten, and feel like I'm SUPPOSED to eat?

Training myself in two-hour increments to not eat was a powerful exercise in self-control which did as much for me mentally as it did physically. After researching long-term fasting and learning about its benefits, I started practicing seventy-two-hour fasts. It was phenomenal! Wow did I feel good, and it worked, boy did it ever.

Right around the time you joined me in Fort Myers, I managed to get 15 of the last 25 pounds off! I was within ten pounds of a touchdown, my LIFETIME GOAL. The following month I did it, I hit the number I had struggled to see for so long. I had now gone from two hundred and twenty-five pounds to one hundred and thirty-nine pounds, where I stayed for over six months.

MJ: Then we got the call from your dad saying his doctor just told him he had stage four metastatic throat cancer.

RENEE: Now, I'm stress eating, I'm Cortisol dumping and we haven't been sleeping. I know none of this helps.

MJ: There's also the THC induced munchies, right?

RENEE: Yeah, also not helping, and I've been using a lot of THC for the pain in my head and neck without making sure I have water nearby, with lots of ice to crunch on. It's a mouth feel thing, I guess.

I once tried prepping a bar glass of crushed ice by pouring lemon juice over it and salting the rim. I put a lime on it for visual appeal and a couple of olives on a side plate sprinkled with Tajin. These things have powerful flavors including salt and ice for hydration which are all key elements in keeping away from THC munchies. I have to have them waiting next to me BEFORE I use THC because after, well, I just don't bother and go straight to the pantry.

MJ: Your level of stress is a lot different than mine because yours directly impacts you on a relationship level. I have a relationship with him too, don't get me wrong, but he's your dad.

You were like, why am I doing this? Why am I eating like this, why am I gaining this kind of weight? I, as a student, would come back to the teacher with her own words of wisdom and remind you, stress as a whole has been working against us.

RENEE: I'm fluctuating anywhere from eight to sixteen pounds so it's not terrible and like you, I never seem to gain more than twenty pounds. Our behaviors and lifestyle are just too ingrained now to let them slip. I'm at the point where not following my own program feels immoral. I can't do it for long without fixing things. It almost feels like my boat, we get rocky a lot, but we don't sink and if we roll the wrong way our keel puts us back on top quickly. I trust you've seen my efforts with the program and believe I've performed well under the circumstances?

MJ: I have, and I do. There were plenty of times while trying to get your dad to gain weight, we'd go to the buffet at Golden Corral. Back in the day, Golden Corral was a big treat for me. It would be nothing for me to have two plates of food in just one trip. Going back several times happened a lot and I'd probably finish with half a pecan pie by myself.

RENEE: Oh yes, you're gonna talk about the pecan pie moment, speak on little grasshopper! I love this story, and it excites me having been there with you in the moment.

MJ: Anyway, thinking back to how I used to eat at Golden Corral, it took discipline for me to come back to the table with only one plate for my meal, followed by a simple salad. I ended my trips to the buffet with one or two SMALL PIECES of dessert.

RENEE: We also make sure we sit at the end where the salads are. Don't sit yourself in front of the dessert bar. I mean, why would you want to abuse yourself that way? Sit at the salad bar end, it helps trust me!

MJ: We went there the other day to have a nice salad and a small plate of protein. We stayed away from the carbohydrate choices because why give them twenty bucks each to eat the cheap stuff right? Fill up on the expensive roasted beef or baked chicken without sugary sauces and glaze. I got a small sliver of pecan pie and a bite of blueberry cobbler. I enjoyed the cobbler, but halfway through the pecan pie I pushed it away. I was done.

That my friends, was a first ever!

RENEE: Well, let's start with the serving sizes you brought back to the table. I believe the cobbler was quite small, wasn't it? It was in one of the tiny, dessert bowls not much bigger than what I would use to put my soy sauce in for sushi. When I used to hit the dessert bar at Golden Corral, I would go get the soup bowls for my dessert instead and a big soup spoon too. Let me just say, you should stick to the little soy sauce dipping dishes for dessert, even if it means you go back several times.

MJ: I came back with the smallest pieces of cobbler and pie. The little sushi dipping saucers would hold no more.

RENEE: So, your serving sizes on each were minimal?

MJ: Yes. I finished the cobbler and had two bites of the pecan pie. You know pecan pie is a weakness of mine, and I pushed it away. It was too much; I was done, and I don't think I've ever experienced a desire to push away from anything at the table before in my life, especially not from pecan pie.

RENEE: I watched you do it and it looked like it wasn't even hard, like you were actually just full, and you pushed it back.

MJ: That's exactly what happened, the whole "just push away" thing in the beginning is always hard. It gets easier because your body does start telling you to push away. You don't have the same space inside your belly or the same desire anymore.

End of Transcript

"You just got to have will power." I'm sure each one of us has heard this phrase, ad nauseum. Have you ever heard of the brain as a muscle? What if I told you it responds like a muscle to training just like your biceps? IT DOES. There is a specific area in your brain called the Anterior Mid Cingulate Cortex or your aMCC, and it needs to get a workout and train as much if not more than your glutes.

Athletes don't just hop on the court or field and go all in. They have a process. First they must do warm up activities before they even practice what they do. After a warm up they do practice drills and other exercises. When coach thinks they're ready they do trial runs or scrimmages and the like. The point is, they begin with a lot of warming up and getting ready while they build up their individual strengths needed for their sport.

Your aMCC is the brain's control center for willpower. Research is ongoing but scientists backed with heavy data are coming to describe it in terms of "the will to persist." Maybe it's important to "use it or lose it" then yeah?

Your aMCC is most active when you push yourself outside your comfort zone. When people do things they don't want to do like resist temptation, add a few hours of exercise, go for a walk; anything you don't want to do, the grey matter of your aMCC gets bigger and stronger!

Interestingly, research also suggests that the aMCC is smaller and less active in obese people which implies a lower aMCC size may relate to greater difficulty in resisting temptation and maintaining self-control. Athletes have a bigger aMCC obviously as they regularly challenge themselves outside their comfort zones. Those of us who view their lives as particularly challenged and then overcome those challenges have an even larger, more active aMCC than the athletes.

There you have it folks! The key to every great work out is to work out with your brain first and foremost. Just like a ball player or a runner, you must build your muscle with warm-ups, practice, and scrimmage. Try to view difficult tasks as opportunities to set you apart from others. When you change your perspective from "This is hard" to "Not everyone can do this," it shifts from a sense of personal struggle to recognizing the challenge for others as well.

So start with something that sucks or that you suck at and tell your inner coach you're not failing because every time you even attempt to exercise or exercise self-control, you win. You win each time you attempt something even if you fail because you're building and flexing your brains aMCC. Remember though, it's not about just doing more work, it has to be the work you don't want to do.

Also, let us not forget, willpower cannot replace discipline, and the two words are not interchangeable. The words differ in how they help you achieve goals.

Willpower is defined by the ability to resist short-term temptations or impulses in favor of long-term goals. It's MOMENTARY, for overcoming IMMEDIATE challenges such as walking out of the grocery store today without the oatmeal cookies. You only gotta say no once till you're out of the store.

Discipline is about creating consistent ROUTINES and structures to support your goals over time such as making a list before you shop and avoiding problem areas of the supermarket in the first place. It involves STICKING TO HABITS even when motivation or willpower fades, making positive actions more AUTOMATIC.

Let's play a scenario and I'm going to use my favorite store we have here for this. Publix is set up to have most of our necessities on each perimeter wall. The back wall is the frozen and fresh meats, the butcher, the fish, etcetera. The wall to the left of the front door goes from pharmacy back to all dairy, breads, and spreads and bottled water. As you go towards the center and start looking in the aisles, you get household goods and personal care on into snack foods and soda.

Off to the right of the front door is the hot deli, the bakery, on into fresh produce. Aisles leading from the right side to center go from coffee and tea to cereals, baking needs and staples. Right next to the staples like flour, oil, and salt are several candy aisles. (*They aren't dumb it's all strategically placed.*) I have discovered I need to avoid the right side of my store as much as possible. The ice cream is down one of those aisles as well. So I have a map.

I shop with a list, and I know to turn left immediately upon entering the store to grab my dairy and bread. I can then make a counter-clockwise path where I pick up chicken, steak, and fish along the back wall until I arrive at the produce section on the right side again, but WAY back from the candy and bakery. I retrace my steps along the back wall to get my staples in an aisle because the candy is closer to the front.

I've been doing things this way for so long now I don't even think about it anymore, my feet just turn left of their own accord. Bakery? Wait, we have a bakery here? I have mostly forgotten, and I rarely think of it. This is an example of my "supportive habit" which requires discipline and cuts my need for willpower in half at least.

There will be days when you just don't have it. If you screw up today it's OK. Be gentle and kind to yourself and just start again at the very next possible moment.

Remember your purpose. Why have you come here, to this point where you considered making these changes? Your purpose can be used to make discipline natural, effortless. So you slipped on a banana split an hour before bed, now you will take steps to mitigate the damage by drinking water and taking a walk around your block before tucking in. I think my biggest point here is if willpower fails you, revisit your purpose. When you f*ck up, BUCK UP and fix it ASAP.

Perhaps you were bored, or you stayed up too late, which caused your body to crave more calories and sugar. The next time you cave in and eat something you shouldn't, stop yourself at the halfway point or before and put it away. Go brush your teeth and go do something for twenty minutes to distract yourself. If its later in the evening try just going to bed, choosing sleep over snacks when you feel the need for revenge bedtime procrastination is a champion move!

There are strategies to help you with bedtime procrastination, and they all involve routines designed to alleviate a sense of lost "free-time." Reclaiming your daytime hours for "me-time" is central to developing a consistent sleep routine as well as setting limits on digital devices.

Absolutely schedule personal time earlier by intentionally carving out time during your day for activities you enjoy so you don't feel the need to steal time at night. Try making a schedule for yourself for an entire day. Schedule each hour and stick to it. If it works out, use it again or tweak it, write it down, I'm sure there's space in your journal.

Boredom is a huge problem for myself and for a lot of people I'd surmise. I once heard someone say, "If you're bored you're boring." Harsh, maybe, but it resonated with me and if I could remember where I heard it, I would tell you so you could slap them rather than me.

It's easy to become "bored." We can be bored with our fitness routines, with our kitchen, with the provisions in our house and with life in general. I find this to be particularly true at the gym or while working out. The only fitness routines I had ever actually engaged in revolved around the typical stuff. There were fitness guru videos, trainers taking my money at the gym, going for a run in my neighborhood, these things would just get recycled in my life as I waited for their individual boredom quotient to go down.

In the past I found a certain kind of entertainment in studying my body and paying close attention to it as I worked on the machines. I would amuse myself with the sensations and changes my body would experience, you know, living in the moment. This stopped working for me after a while and I got bored. Now it seems I can only get myself to "work out" by doing things I love.

I love kayaking and long walks. I love hiking and rock climbing. I just want to be outdoors, so we try to find ways of working/working out, outside. This has been very good for us and today we may be ready to bounce back to the gym again. Remaining flexible with yourself is important I think. Don't be afraid to experiment and move around within your program whatever your program looks like to you. Experimenting with new things helps keep boredom at bay and nurtures passion. It's very hard to be bored and passionate at the same time. As a disclaimer, experiment with all things from a place of respect.

We write about everything in a journal as I keep suggesting you all do. It remains important throughout this journey. Not only does it help identify things you're passionate about, but it also helps you identify and work with your habits. Journaling helps us keep things like workouts compact and effective. By tracking your experiences this way, particularly new experiences, you will more readily be in touch with how the new things make you feel.

Doing it all for love sounds so cliché and not practical. Previously when people said this to me, my response generally sounded something like,

"OK. Yes, I know. Do what you're passionate about, do what you love, but what does that look like? What is a practical application of this?" Doing what you love always sounded so ridiculous because who really has the time or the ability to do what they love and how does doing what I love help me to lose weight?

That's just it! You have to figure it out, make time and in every situation you've got to CREATE new loves and new passions. I GREW my passion; I didn't always obsess over food and nutrition like I do today. I didn't get like this until I found ways to connect with my nourishment, and once I got turned on to this newfound connection to food, I had to change the way I thought about what and how I eat.

For example, I began to really focus hard on the RITUAL of food and its preparation as a way to grow RESPECT for my cuisine and the art of fine dining. Fine dining does not necessarily mean breaking the bank on a five-star restaurant. I do fine dining every day at home.

I figured if I was going to constantly be thinking about food anyway I might as well really think about it until there's nothing left to consider. I wondered how much professional chefs thought about food and I concluded they never stopped, and each serving was planned or agonized over to the very moment of swallowing.

That's what we do, right? When we try not to eat, or go on a diet, or lose weight, we suddenly only think about food. OMG, is it lunch time yet? Is this a good snack?

Well, if you're gonna have it on your mind all the time anyway, make it work for you. Each time you think about your meals try to think of them in new terms. Use the obsession over food to fight boredom, but not by eating first. First think in GREAT DETAIL about what you want to eat. Here's a little creative exercise to demonstrate this idea.

SCENARIO

For breakfast today I want pancakes and sausage. I have two different kinds of batter. I wonder if one is better than the other, so I read both boxes for ingredients and notice one has cocoa butter and the other has canola oil.

I thought cocoa butter sounded much more delicious than oil, so I decided to research cocoa butter and canola oil and low and behold, cocoa butter is significantly better for you. Ok, now, what would I like to put on those pancakes? There are so many options, and I like them all. I prefer having my toppings run all across the pancakes and watching it cascade in a rich, amber colored flow off the side of a tall, fluffy stack. Jelly and other spreadables are eliminated from the options, they don't flow.

Do I want syrup, honey, or agave? I need to think about this part a little harder. I want something richer and sweeter than agave and agave doesn't have the amber glow. I've narrowed it down to syrup or honey and I'm stuck. I love them both and to me they are equally rich and sweet. Hmmmm, I could just hurry and pick one. Screw it, syrup is easier because I can flip the top and squeeze to watch it flow.

No. Stop. Think about this and get PASSIONATE about it! OK, the honey doesn't flow like the syrup, and it is stickier, so I end up using more. It is all natural though, and without any of those fake, toxic chemicals. Oh wait, I also have true maple syrup from Canada. It's expensive and lovely, rich and golden, sweet and flavorful. I love the smell and feel of it. The squeezy syrup smells weird and the maple smells amazing and goes great with my coffee. Maple syrup it is.

Am I going to have anything else or just the pancakes? Fruit sounds more in line suddenly, rather than sausage since it is so colorful, refreshing, and lighter than sausage. However, it is Saturday morning, and I have all day to work it off, and I really like the salt with my sweet. The bacon could be lighter perhaps. Hmmm, I wonder which one has less nitrates and stuff because I heard that's not good. After a quick google to find out which one has less harmful stuff, I got caught in a rabbit hole. Apparently nitrates and nitrites are not the same, but are used interchangeably in the food industry and both are common in sausage and bacon. Lots of learning happened here.

Nitrites are three times stronger than nitrates. Nitrates are also in healthy vegetables and the chemistry learning involved took me right back to high school science. Suffice it to say, I was left with the idea we should eat our lean processed meats with veggies and fatty processed meats by themselves. Ok. Both bacon and sausage are fatty processed meats, and I also learned last week I shouldn't mix my sugars with proteins.

I elected to slice some strawberries and add blackberries and raspberries to a side bowl of unsweetened, unflavored Greek yogurt. Yogurt tastes amazing with honey drizzled on it. I like my hot food hot and my cold food cold, not in between and the two should not mix, that's just who I am. So, I prepare the berries first. I love pretty things and one of the main reasons I spend so much time in restaurants is because I love the ambiance and the lighting, and the way food is presented like art on the plates. You know what, I am gonna try that myself, so I google stuff. "How to make a presentation with berries and yogurt."

Now that I've seen very appealing pictures, I realize I want a fancy bowl to put it in and you know, while I'm at it, I want my entire breakfast to be presented fancy. I proceed to spend twenty minutes or more finding my nicest serving ware and the perfect yogurt and fruit bowl. I look around and notice the morning sun on my back porch. It's a glorious morning and birds are singing. I recently picked up this cute little patio dining set I haven't even used yet, so I think I will set up my perfect dishes out there.

It turns out to be a great idea. I step back to view my table setting, complete with a nice sheet doing double duty as a linen tablecloth and a nice dish towel holding second as a linen napkin. I feel like something is missing still. I noticed the weeds in my back yard are overgrown but hey, they sure put up some pretty flowers. I pick a handful and hunt down a bud vase for a centerpiece. Turning on my relaxing music, I know this is gonna be a great morning and a great breakfast.

I go back inside and do my best to copy the fancy slicing and shape-making with my berries for the yogurt. Hmm, the picture looks fresher, what's different? I dig to the bottom of my veggie drawer and there is some parsley almost ready to be tossed, I find a piece that is still good so I can garnish my fruit bowl. Perfect! The bowl waits for me in the fridge.

I've always been good at pancakes, and we know it does require a bit of practice and some technique. I go to lubricate my pan and again I stop to think. What should I grease my pan with? So many choices and after another twenty minutes or so with Google and my thoughts, I decide I want pure Irish butter because it's supposed to be better for me than all of these seed and/or vegetable oils. I also realize I have put so many special things into this meal already, OIL doesn't seem to do it justice now. The Irish butter seems more special and elegant for this meal I'm working so hard on.

As my pan is heating, I grab the last, salvageable sprig of parsley. I sprinkle a bit of powdered sugar across the plate for presentation and realize sugar is not good. I Google a replacement and vow to get a brand of powdered monk fruit or erythritol next time, or better yet, skip this step all together. Maybe I'll dress up my plate with a pretty, paper doily under the pancakes for that white, lacy look. A nice citrus slice like orange, lemon, or lime or all three would be beautiful!

I sit at the table and pull my chair up and as I start to engage with utensils, I stop to look at what I have made for myself. I close the back door and the windows because everyone else in the house is noisy, and I want to be present in this moment I have prepared for myself. I put a lot of work into this, and nothing should take even a piece of joy from my enJOYment.

END OF SCENARIO

Are you, our readers feeling this yet? This kind of process can help you in so many ways. It takes up a lot of space and time in our minds and it's space and time you already dedicate to thinking about eating anyway. It can distract, teach, delay satisfaction and impulses. Do this for EVERYTHING you eat and prepare. Start with just one thing or one meal in your day and build from there.

Figure 13: Preparing for a beautiful meal!

Figure 14: MJ doing her iconic pose on the levy of Lake Okeechobee 2022.

Figure 15: MJ doing the iconic pose on Bourbon Street New Orleans 2024.

Chapter 5

CORE ESSENTIALS

WHAT MAKES IT ALL WORK

"I can't even say it was mindset really, because I wasn't in a good place in my mind at all, I just did it. I took the plan you gave me and went with it."–

MJ Cutsinger

MJ asked me if I had a strategy, which I can't honestly say for sure I did, but my mom's favorite advice to me was frequently,

"Fake it till you make it." My favorite slogan became a mantra for me, applicable to all things and my number one rule.

I remember way back, when my part of the weight loss journey truly began, I was pregnant with my second child and my OB/GYN told me I needed to lose weight. I freaked out on him, crying I said,

"What do you mean I have to LOSE weight, I'm pregnant I'm supposed to gain weight!" He explained to me, at two hundred and twenty-five pounds with a diagnosis of gestational diabetes, I would be jeopardizing the health of my unborn child if I didn't lose weight.

He sent me to a dietician/nutritionist who gave me this food journal in which I had to write down absolutely everything going into my mouth as well as what I did during the day for physical activity. Like mom said,

"If you bite it, you write it." In order to monitor my body's response to insulin injections, I meticulously logged and calculated the nutritional information from each label into my book.

I remember thinking how hard this all was and how I had no clue what I was doing, which stressed me out because my baby's health was on the line. I started thinking of my log book as a bible of sorts. It was hard evidence of participation in my doctor's program.

My body was already extremely insulin resistant at this point and my doctors were sure I wasn't cooperating. I began to get angry, and this little book became a way for me to study and understand this whole new lifestyle and diet I had to follow. You could say I started a self-study program to independently observe the effects of each meal or snack on my well-being.

I think back with no small amount of pride to the last appointment I had with my dietician/nutritionist because I gave her a full discourse on better choices and what I had learned by trial and error. She even asked me if I ever thought about taking courses. I laughed and said something like,

"I'm just feeling scared and overwhelmed because I'm doing my best and my blood sugars aren't responding to the insulin. I don't know what I'm doing so I'm taking mom's advice and I'm trying to fake it till I make it."

After nine months of rigorous studying and being more disciplined than I've ever been, I felt as though I had already attended school and should be certified. By the end of my pregnancy I felt a new purpose in life, and being so disciplined about it was exciting.

Each time I was rewarded by the pleasure my discipline enabled, I now know I was getting a rush of dopamine. When my son was born, I quite easily decided to continue with this new way of life. A fire had been lit and refused to be extinguished. Fake it till you make it.

Obviously, not everyone has a reason so patently life or death which is a good thing believe me. My son was born with kidney problems and was ill for the first five years of his life until a surgery fixed what it could. He's in his twenties now and has eighty-three percent left of his kidney function. The doctors have all informed me it wasn't anything I did or didn't do, but as a mom I can't not wonder. We moms can really do things to ourselves with guilt. Now I transform my helpless feelings of guilt into helpful actions.

While I'm sharing all I've learned with others, I seem to get reminded on a regular basis about giving myself some grace. So I'm saying, you should be giving yourself a little grace, take your diet and health seriously but don't take yourself so seriously.

Make an effort to minimize the pressure you feel about it and refrain from paying too much attention to the established narratives such as,

"Calories in vs. calories out" or

"You just gotta exercise more." Yes exercise is important, no one is belaboring this point. There is, however, more to it. Few things are rarely so simple and focusing solely on calories and exercise won't work because it's not a purpose. It's not meaningful.

I think flexibility is essential and understanding there isn't one key for everyone, your key is unique and as individual as you are. Your ability to keep an open mind and to hold forgiveness for yourself and space to fail sometimes but, without excuses is paramount.

Preparation is a significantly underrated element to something like weight loss because it directly impacts consistency, decision making, and the ability to sustain healthy habits; all of these being core essentials.

Preparedness prevents impulsive choices and responses to daily life, thereby reducing the likelihood of resorting to unhealthy, convenient options like fast food or processed snacks during busy moments. Preparing your ROUTINES is equally as important as preparing your meals because this is how you make something so much a part of your life you don't even think about it anymore. Routines help to ensure important components are not skipped, like preparing special water before a fast, which is essential.

Organizing your schedule, meals, and workout plans lowers stress. We've already discussed how preparation encourages mindful eating with an awareness of portion sizes, calorie intake, and food quality for consistently healthier choices. We even suggest preparing ahead of time for mindfulness in your routines at work. I tell my friends to map out for the week what and where they will be going for breaks and for lunch during the day.

If you work on the twelfth floor, walk down all or halfway before taking an elevator. When you come back, park in the furthest possible space away from your destination and walk up as many floors as you can before riding the rest in an elevator. This all takes a plan because you have to factor in extra time. You may also wish to purchase things to augment your personal program such as a giant yoga ball and ankle or wrist weights.

Plan to bring your arm and leg weights or to buy an extra set for under your desk at work. You can wear them on your wrists while you type. What a workout! If you bring the biggest yoga ball to work, you can sit on it for a good part of the day and get a complete core workout. Holding yourself up on a ball engages your entire core muscles for a trimmer waist and stronger back.

We even suggest a contingency plan for those days you rush out the door without your prepared meal. Do some local research and map out a list of restaurants or other providers of sustenance. You'll need to do some research on who has the best of the bad choices out there. When I last checked, it was Chipotle with their "fresher" food options. Preparedness on so many levels is essential right down to preparing to "fight" for your decisions within your circle of influence.

As with all the answers, you will need to do some tweaking to find which ones fit with you. Achieving a sustainable change of habits happens gradually by easy corrections.

I think we are too rushed and too hurried and we're not taking time with our food. Seriously. At all. I mean, food and eating in general has become a side dish concept. We DO the rest of life while gobbling up our food which IS LIFE.

Basically, we should be taking the time to have a sexy and romantic dinner for two even if it's by the light of your cell phone over a pack of Seven Eleven donuts. Please don't eat those. If you do, get the prettiest napkin you can find to spread out like a comforter over your center console and the Seven also carries roses.

Buy yourself some flowers for your parking lot romance, don't cheap out on yourself with nothing but a pack of yucky donuts. Go all the way. Don't just fall off the wagon, jump off with both feet. Make food a relationship status because if the moment is special enough to break all of your own rules then make it really special.

I am regularly informed I possess the ability to re-frame concepts in a manner others can comprehend, or to share perspectives they had not previously been able to appreciate. MJ tells me frequently how my perspective was essential for her to experience such a change. By continually emphasizing positive elements and adding to a healthy life rather than focusing on what to remove, we are tapping into the pleasure center. So it automatically feels better.

We hope to leave followers and readers with some new keys and a support system. You can subscribe to our e-mail list, and we will assist you on this journey for as long as we are able. Why? It's my passion. It's our passion and we want to share it. Learning is another passion for me. Now, we're all learning success comes with work you can never quit on, particularly the mental work. If you don't fail occasionally, all you're learning is that success comes easy so just keep showing up for yourself.

CONTACT US:

mjcutsinger@gmail.com

evesironbutterfly@gmail.com

www.terratheoria.com

Figure 16: Renee before and after photos of her journey.

Figure 17: MJ preparing for the best sushi in West Palm Beach at Go Sushi.

Much love Sing & Sylvia!

Chapter 6

Essential Ingredients of Success

"Magic is the art of thinking, not strength or language."–
Christopher Paolini

People often equate passion with sex and romance. However, passion encompasses much more, just as love is deeper than its four letters. A passion for my own body was not something I thought of until a much later era in my life. MJ says the same. We grew up in the eighties, there wasn't a lot of our current awareness regarding things like body positivity.

In fact, I was positively tortured by kids in school, and I saw myself as awkward, chubby, and mousy. As I grew, I surpassed the other girls and boys in height and build and my opinion in the mirror stayed pretty low. MJ experienced similar circumstances, and we are by no means alone in this. It took me all the way to fifty before I had the presence of mind to ask myself why and the spirit to stand in the mirror long enough for the answers.

Why do I not feel love and care towards myself and why do I struggle with seeing myself naked in my bathroom? My body had brought two amazing people into this world, and I was married to people who truly enjoyed my physical appearance, why was I incapable of feeling beautiful? I had a passion all right, a passion for hating on myself. It wasn't until I began experiencing physical limitations due to Multiple Sclerosis that I began to really try to appreciate myself and my body for its abilities. I had to start losing to win I guess, and it became my springboard into the pool of self-love which in turn became self-passion.

Nurturing a sense of passion for all things inside and outside of my body led to studies, research, and education. It still took me a hot minute to start with all of the necessary and practical applications but, here we are.

Figure 18: Unforgettable Valentines Dinner on Tandapata Cusco Peru

Passion

Transcripts Audio Journal

"Cooking is not about perfection but about passion on a plate."– Unknown

RENEE: Were we talking about the passion for food while eating my eggs the other day? What were we saying?

MJ: Oh passion! You could taste the passion in them. I wanted to make a related point in the book.

RENEE: Oh, yeah you were telling me a story about how you like watching me cook because you can see the passion I put into every detail.

"It doesn't matter what you're cooking," you said. "it's like watching you do magic with each step in the process."

MJ: I was imagining what you're cooking, and I was like, why so serious, and you said,

"Well because whenever I cook something, when I cook anything, I swear I actually FEEL magic going into the food from my hands."

RENEE: Was THC involved in those eggs?

MJ: *(laughing around a large mixing bowl of salad.)* No! You said,

"You need to understand we put our energy into our food right from the beginning when we start with the planning of the meal."

RENEE: I think that's a little esoteric and fantastical even for me. I think you were actually saying something about how I get very focused on it.

MJ: I think you said it was spiritual. That's right, you said it's a spiritual thing for you and I said well food is a very spiritual experience, but we used another word when we talked about this before.

RENEE: Yeah, we used another word right before spiritual; first we said it was serious.

MJ: Was it serious?

RENEE: *(Laughing)* I don't know but passion did come up. It's a passionate thing and it's a serious thing. If people heal themselves to a point where they can discern all the intricate flavors and smells like we do now, maybe they would have a transformative experience with their food.

Having the ability to smell and taste things most people don't recognize puts its own spin on food appreciation, like being able to identify salt or sugar when you're not supposed to know. I believe my senses are sharper and my palate more sensitive after removing an excess of things from my diet such as sugars, salt, and additives.

The realization I could smell hidden ingredients in my food was a major catalyst in starting my journey to author a book about us. I thought everyone should know what they are missing.

MJ: That's what started it, because I was thinking of the delicate aroma of the steaming Brussels sprouts with a tea bag underneath it, I was amazed, I could taste the green tea alright.

RENEE: And I asked you, do you feel you would have been able to taste such a subtle thing, these unfamiliar flavors had you not healed yourself to this point?

MJ: There's no way I could have, and bam! There we go, I wanted to recreate this moment because I felt it could be helpful in explaining passion.

RENEE: Indeed!

End of Transcript

Figure 19: MJ was awarded 2nd best dismount for sandboarding at Huacachina Oasis in Peru. Let it be noted that Renee holds the record!

Goals and rewards are **essential ingredients** to success without a doubt! Think... **Dopamine**... remember, be your own butler, set yourself up today for tomorrow's success and make that **discipline** be your dopamine. You'll set **goals** and earn **rewards** at each milestone, including one-week, two-week, three-week, and one-month intervals. You'll find it's incredibly helpful to enlist friends or family as **coaches** or trainers especially for the first six months.

If you are among those blessed to have someone in your life you can call at two A.M. when you feel like going off the rails on a bad choice bender, get prepared to get out of the driver's seat and hand your newly appointed "sponsor" the keys if necessary.

You and this other person will pre-plan or design escape hatches, plans B and C which will be your coping mechanisms to use just in case. Maybe the two of you can **plan** to show up on each other's doorstep for an impromptu karaoke night or decide to start a book club, anything to lovingly distract the other from derailing.

If you don't have someone this close and willing, join a **support** group somewhere and call an actual sponsor. Twelve Step programs for weight loss are a thing. If you really can't share as a deeply entrenched loner, you'll have to find other avenues but find them in advance!

Don't wait until you're at the critical moment of breaking your hard-won streak of fantastic habits! Remember, being hungry is not bad. It can be **uncomfortable,** but it's important to distinguish between feeling bad and feeling uncomfortable, as they are often confused.

Consider the approach of Olympians. **Training** involves **preparation**, which includes daily, repeated runs or timed runs without partners to prepare for a race. When the Olympic track and field gold medalist first thought about being an Olympian, they knew they would have to train and make sacrifices to the gods of comfort. They had to learn how to train, which meant they would also be training to be uncomfortable until their body adjusted.

They needed special shoes and equipment. They had coaches telling them when to sleep and when to train and nutritionists managing what and how they eat. It is an incredibly disciplined way to live as you can imagine and you're going to do the same thing. This is training my friends, training, and preparation. You are going to be a gold medalist in managing your health.

It takes sincere **desire** to discipline yourself to reach your goals, and you don't have to be an Olympian to qualify for desire. Would you call desire another word for **passion**? I would. It's your earnest desire, a purpose that will see you through the discipline.

If you Google statistics on weight loss failure due to poor discipline versus other reasons, you will likely find limited information. However, some insights can be drawn. Poor **adherence** (A.K.A discipline) to diets and exercise plans is a major reason for failure. Studies report adherence rates as low as 28-40% with lack of **motivation**, unrealistic expectations, and poor **self-confidence** being key factors.

About 80-95% of people regain the weight they lose within one or two years after reaching their goal, illustrating once again how the work never stops. I also found in statistics the strongest predictor of long-term weight loss success is the ability to achieve a greater weight reduction in the first six months, which is why we encourage you to enlist your closest people to help. Individuals who adhere closely to their programs during this period are more likely to maintain weight loss over two years.

MJ has been at or above her goal by a mere 10 or 15 pounds for almost five years now. She lost seventy-eight pounds in the first five months. Having the discipline to sustain adherence to your plans, particularly in your early days, is critical for achieving goals and maintaining them for the long term.

Internalizing and **accepting** your new way of living and establishing a creed for yourself is like making sure you have clean counters and utensils in your kitchen before preparing a meal. A creed is a short, deeply personal set of guiding **principles** or **beliefs** and is more about values than actions such as, "I believe in honesty, resilience and continuous growth." Write your own creed at the front of your journal.

At the front of your journal, you should also include a **mission statement**. A mission statement is a concise declaration of your **purpose** and direction. It can include what you do, why you do it, and how you do it. For example, "I am committed to helping others while maintaining my health and personal growth."

For extra credit and serious commitment, consider drafting your own **manifesto**, a more detailed and passionate document often outlining your philosophy, **rules,** and plans for action. I'm sure you'll recollect-- **words** have super powers so be inspirational to yourself. Maybe something like,

"I reject negativity and procrastination. I will prioritize my health and seek support towards my goal of (insert here) on my own terms."

If you want something structured and flexible, a mission statement is a solid choice. If you want something powerful and motivational, a manifesto may be best. Please don't leave these out of your essential ingredients. Taking the time to do this and a few other things in your book is a first step, a first promise to yourself. It's a **promise** you make in your head as you reinforce it by **writing** it down *(signed and notarized for the win)* and no doubt you will have read it aloud once or twice.

Your self-promise will be imagined, written, seen, heard, and when you go to the notary and seal it, you will have tasted your envelope and heard your Notary thump her stamp on a hard copy of a **contract** you've made with yourself. Every single one of your senses has gotten involved now, you've taken considerable time to do these things and spent money. YOU ARE INVESTED.

This brings us to the final ingredient, the third D in my "Three D's." When you find your **Desire,** you practice **Discipline** with your habits and arrive at better **Decisions**. I consider this to be the cornerstone of my approach, my KEY ingredients.

Figure 20: MJ getting ready to climb aboard the Amtrak for the first time for a cross-country adventure. What fun it was!

Chapter 7

A Map: Your 1ˢᵗ Steps to Journey

"Don't speak negatively about yourself, even as a joke. Your body doesn't know the difference. Words are energy and they cast spells, that's why it's called spelling. Change the way you speak about yourself, and you can change your life." – Bruce Lee

Practical step-by-step guide.

Step 1- Entertaining the idea

If this book is in your hand you've taken a step! You have already decided to make changes and you've begun looking for things to facilitate your new life. You made decisions that led you to this book, whether by chance or choice. Clearly, healing was already on your mind. You have continued reading to this point, so you're open-minded enough to entertain our guidance.

If you didn't skip the journaling assignments from our previous chapter you've already passed go once, collected your two hundred in monopoly money and if you got it notarized, you landed on free parking. You're ahead of the game.

Journaling should be considered the first step, although it was not initially included as such. Sometimes action takes precedence over contemplation, so we wanted to share the option, reflect on your journal *(your soul contract)* or choose to bypass this step. Either way, you've already come this far! Look at you go right? The first step already feels like five so congratulations you motivated monarch!

Step 2- What is your driving force today?

Understanding what you want and why you want it is crucial. This step requires time and thought, which many people tend to rush through because thinking is not an action. This is a huge misconception because you need a purpose–why do you intend to lose weight? Why do you intend to shape different habits and what will the new habits look like? Instead of writing generally about better health, be specific. For instance, state a plan to lose fifteen pounds within four to six months to potentially lower blood pressure and reduce medications. Be ridiculously specific in your intentions. What will you change or do differently today to achieve tomorrow's goal and maintain progress into next week?

Take the necessary time to analyze your intentions PLEASE, but without getting bogged down in overthinking. Consider runners preparing for a race—they focus intently on their goal, ready to spring into action at the sound of the starting gun. Similarly, you must prepare yourself mentally and physically.

Can you imagine, you and your friend are walking a few blocks after your lunch break, just casually cruising a shortcut through the park, talking about the latest Netflix series in between bites of your Wendy's frosty when a starting gun goes off. What do you and your friend do? You drop to the ground scared for your life, your frosty is in the dirt and you have grass stains on your work clothes. You're certainly not posed in a sprinter's position on the starting line are you? You're completely unprepared to run.

Meanwhile, your coworkers are winning the company sponsored race and a five-hundred-dollar bonus. You didn't read the memo, wear the right attire, or do warm-up exercises. Would you expect yourself to drop your frosty and start sprinting with everyone else and would you expect yourself not to fall in your work shoes? Would you expect yourself to win the race? No, probably not so don't skip the warm ups or getting yourself prepared and don't take so long getting prepared you never show up. Get ready. Get set. GO.

Can you remember what thought first went through your mind right before you decided to open this book? Did you look at MJ on the cover and say to yourself, "No f@#k'n way! What the hell…what surgery did she get?" Were you thinking anything along these lines? That my friends, is called disbelief in the power to change.

Don't worry, no judgement here merely observations. MJ and I are still shocked at times. Frequently while authoring this book, we had to stop and hold our hearts in our loving hands because the power of disbelief is strong. You must prepare yourself for this and whatever you do…DO NOT DOUBT THE POWER OF WHAT YOU BELIEVE.

Do you believe in why you want to make these changes? Is it to fit into your bestie's dumb bridesmaid's dress or is it literally life and death such as saving your unborn child due to gestational diabetes? If it's in the neighborhood of the dress, it is no less important, but you better honestly believe in your reason. If it's a "dumb dress" your desire is probably not for the dress.

Maybe you love your bestie and her joy on this day lights up your world so why upset the party with your feelings about it? Perhaps it's more about the other bridesmaids because they fit into their cute dresses perfectly and you don't want to be out like that?

If you are masculine and the other groomsmen get together for a tuxedo fitting, do you feel some kind of way about being out of shape and needing a special fitting? All of it is valid if you BELIEVE. You don't need a lifesaving reason, but you will need a solid purpose you can get emotionally attached to. You don't need a lifetime goal to start with; a short-term goal will do fine for now. Just as the saying "a rolling stone gathers no moss" is scientifically correct, what we lack in purpose and motivation can be augmented with MOMENTUM. Sometimes the doing helps us believe.

Step 3- Analyze your habits

It is essential to thoroughly examine your habits, evaluate them, and identify those which are counterproductive. These habits significantly impact whether you achieve your goals. Not all habits stem from deep-seated issues; some are simply formed over time due to circumstances. Establishing good habits requires discipline and planning and you want to set your life up as if you work for yourself. Be your own monkey butler by making things as easy as you can for yourself going forward.

Set reminders for yourself, document all your habits, and make a conscious effort to implement the good ones like leaving your keys in the same predetermined spot every time. We've all felt an intense rush of relief *(dopamine)* when we run out late for work and find our keys where they belong. Habits. They can make us or break us. Take a minute or two understanding yourself by focusing on your motivations and developing constructive habits so you can set a solid foundation for success.

Your local Hobby Lobby has an entire inventory of motivational quotes for adorning your walls, pillows, or even bar top accoutrements. Quotes like "Live, Laugh, Love" or "Breathe, Believe, Achieve" are everywhere. I used to think how trite and laughably over used they are.

In actuality, these little nuggets of wordy, worldly wisdom are golden. Gold leaf may be paper thin, seeming inconsequential but, it is still pure gold. Have you looked at the price of gold per troy ounce lately *(not the regular ounce because the troy ounce is more reliable globally)*? As I'm typing this it is at $3,035.50 per ounce. So analyze why you do it and then **STOP TALKING SH*T ABOUT YOURSELF!** It's a terrible habit and you are **LITERALLY** investing in yourself by the gold standard.

We've all heard the power of the pen is mightier than the sword. Let's examine this along with, "sticks and stones may break our bones, but words hurt worse than anything." It would seem words have a power equal to weapons, they can be used for disassembly or war as in Hitler's "Mein Kampf" which fueled hatred, and anti-Semitism leading to World War II.

They also share the subtle, elegant power of a scalpel, razor sharp and used to elegantly remove anything not serving the body. [9] The American Medical Association Journal of Ethics highlights how scalpels and words are tools to "cure or kill," emphasizing the importance of using them with care and intention to avoid harm. Words can act as instruments of healing as they address emotional wounds and foster deep connections. When used skillfully, words can remove dis-ease *(state of being uneasy)* and save lives.

I no longer laugh at the Hobby Lobby effect all of those ticky-tacky plaques, posters, apple crates, and coffee cups have on my house. I'm putting them wherever I need to be reminded of the power in words. Please, no offense to the Hobby Lobby followers, don't come at me. As it turns out, you were heading the right direction all along.

Lately I've been a fan of "Learn it, Live it, Love it." I like to stick it everywhere in my face along with other things I find inspirational. This has been an actionable step in my approach for a long time now. Today it's inspirational words and thoughts, in the beginning of my journey I used pictures of myself from various, earlier stages in my life. At my heaviest, I was 225 pounds. I put up pictures taken a few years prior when I weighed fifty pounds less and kept going backwards in time to my thinner years. I put those pictures everywhere and I would end up staring, looking or habitually glancing at them all day.

I wanted to remind myself anything is possible, look who I used to be and look where I am now. Back then I thought I was terribly out of shape and fat but, there I was, willing to "give it up" to be the me in those older pictures again. Some of the pictures were just a few years old! How many times have you done that? How many times have you come across older pictures of yourself and thought, "Wow, I used to think I was heavy then, I should be this weight today and I'd feel a lot better?

The exciting part here is this means anything is possible through you, and you can look at pictures for hard evidence. Now you are becoming aware. You can make the changes anytime you choose to look and feel like you did in any of those pictures. They were your reality and can be again. For innumerable reasons you may not have access to old photos of yourself. Try asking your friends. You'd be surprised at some candid photos they took of you.

 I also had pictures from magazines or advertisements of fashions I wanted to wear but didn't feel comfortable in due to my size. I put them everywhere. Seriously, I printed or posted pictures all over my life. I would see them on walls, whiteboards, refrigerator magnets, screen savers, home screens, lock screens, graffiti, etcetera. I even had strategic photos put on a set of dishes I liked to use.

Imagine going back for a third helping while your own face is looking up at you through a shmear of spaghetti sauce and chunky tomatoes, It stopped me at one helping. I hung my size 18 dress pants, which I regularly wore to work, on my dining room wall next to a framed and enlarged, glossy, print of my goal outfit. Inspired by the stark contrast in quality and size of the garments, I found myself yearning for change every day as I sat down for breakfast and dinner, gazing at them side by side on the wall. I decided the outfit would be my first reward.

I weighed myself and took all the necessary measurements to compare them with measurements required for the outfit to fit well. I researched typical weight changes associated with size reductions. I found an estimate suggesting I should account for one size adjustment for every ten to fifteen pounds lost based on body type. Just like that, I gave myself a vision board, a plan, numbers, and a readily achievable goal. Now I needed a plan of action.

Taking time out of my already busy day to mess with these things seemed silly at first and it was kind of a pain in my ass. Today I feel it profoundly helped me, especially in my weaker, less motivated times. Doing these "ridiculous" things set the stage for learning to live with INTENTION and DISCIPLINE.

I analyzed my current habits, reflecting on whether I frequently avoid situations, tasks, or conversations that cause discomfort. I do. I procrastinate, cancel plans, and I'm really good at distracting myself with unrelated activities. Distraction is my personal favorite, but it's hard to do when you completely surround yourself with so many visual reminders of what you're trying to accomplish, and you're looking at them everywhere all day.

Learning these things about myself has been invaluable and MJ used some of the same tools and assessments as I did. We highly recommend the Meyer's-Briggs Type Indicator *(MBTI)* as it helps understand personality traits influencing your coping styles such as introversion or neuroticism. Another good one is DISC Assessment which focuses on behavioral tendencies, offering insights into how you respond to discomfort or stress.

These are both personality profiling tests. You can also use self-awareness and reflection tools such as the Tasha Eurich Test. It's a comprehensive tool to assess your emotions, thoughts, and behaviors, helping you identify patterns like avoidance. This is where I give great thanks to the captain of my blanket fort, my friend Diana for setting us up with such things. You are an awesome friend.

Personality and coping style assessment tests like the Coping Strategies Scale, could be useful to identify whether you rely on active or avoidant strategies by analyzing how you manage stressors in your life. If you are more of a "let me ask my peeps" kind of person, you can use tools like 360-Degree Feedback. It collects feedback from peers or mentors to identify blind spots in your coping mechanisms.

Taking some time with such tools is a highly underrated life hack and you'll be learning commitment and desire. Using at least one is like getting an upgraded ticket for a smoother ride on this journey. Why not take the opportunity to show yourself love and support with such good decision-making tools?

"This is the hardest step." MJ said. "This is where all the what if's come up and make you doubt your ability to commit. You know you gotta just close your eyes and do it. With faith, in yourself, your higher power, your friends, or whatever support you can grasp when you reach out."

Step 4 - Create your plan and go shopping

Before we get into planning meals and food shopping, let's talk about an often-overlooked step, the purge. Clean your kitchen. Spring clean it. Throw out anything expired, unsealed or if freshness is compromised. If you can afford it, purge worn or damaged cookware and dishes. If you have flaking pots and pans get rid of them immediately. When you sit down to eat, open windows and blinds, the pleasing vista makes you take longer at the table and remember you're getting romantic with yourself every time.

Now pick **ONE** of your favorite junk foods or snacks from your collection. Keep it and make the rest go away by donating, gifting, or trashing it. For each discarded item, replace it with vegetables and some fruits. Be sincere about it. The recommendation to keep your one preferred guilty pleasure is based on a balanced approach. Rather than focusing on removing items from your diet, it emphasizes adding

114

healthier options. You can eat whatever you like, but only after consuming sixteen ounces of vegetables first and the healthy options should take up more space than anything else.

This is an important initial step because it provides an opportunity today to motivate you tomorrow. How the heck does eating a whole steamable bag of Brussel sprouts by myself before eating anything else do that you may ask. Well, tomorrow when you see the scale and remember you skipped dessert or only ate half a slice of pie, you'll smile because you chose to fill up on vegetables to avoid overeating other stuff.

The past you *(yesterday)* did the future you *(today's you)* a solid and chose making you happy today as a priority. Now, instead of being angry at yourself for yesterday, you can stand there feeling the dopamine hit of victory today. You have just made discipline a source of excitement, a positive experience.

Making decisions to prioritize yourself ought to be your focus because it directly relates to where motivation is sourced. It is beneficial to look back without regret, to recognize previous actions with appreciation. It turns discipline into a motivating factor.

As for the veggies, they can be fresh or frozen, cooked, or raw. Just make sure they're actually vegetables and not things like corn or tubers such as potatoes and yams. Also, carrots become a starch when you cook them, and raw spinach can cause kidney stones. Make sure you have at least a week's worth of everything on hand because we all have days where we show up as the worst version of ourselves and the last thing you're going to want at the end of it is to run to the store. Advance ordering and auto-shipping healthy options like frozen steamable veggies is a great way to prioritize yourself.

Wouldn't it be sweet if we could also add love notes to ourselves in our delivered packages? Remember how good it feels when your spouse or partner does it? We do it for our kids and why, to make them feel loved and special. It's a dopamine hit. Look into leaving yourself notes wherever you might find them in the not-too-distant future and feel the pleasure in your self-love later. This IS a step. Don't skip it.

Now I want to talk about slowing down. When you get pulled over doing 85-90 in a 45 zone and the cop, ready to arrest you for reckless driving wants to know what your major malfunction is, what can you possibly say? "I'm sorry officer, it's kind of hard to read the signs when you're going 90?" SLOW DOWN! We should all be slowing down in everything we do, yes everything. Whenever you find your nervous system out of whack, the easiest way to regulate yourself is to slow down.

I have a friend who eats fast compulsively. I mentioned it once and she was like,

"You sound like my mother." So I'd wager she's been inhaling her food since childhood. It's funny, but it's not. Some people have a broken hormone switch that doesn't flip off when they've reached satiety. Their bodies never send the "push away" signal which comes from hormones made in your gut.

If you're shoveling enough food to bend your utensils beneath the weight of every scoop, your satiety switch doesn't have time to flip. The hormone regulators don't work fast enough; they take about twenty minutes to reach your brain from your gut. Anything you can use as a speed bump while eating your snacks and meals will help you immensely.

When you take smaller bites and chew longer, you end up doing more work for less volume in your mouth. You naturally consume less and the increased hand to mouth action gives room for a sense of, "Okay, I'm ready to be done now." This means your serving size gets smaller until you begin to be satisfied with a true portion size.

I learned how to eat almost anything with chopsticks. MJ, however, is still learning! Chopsticks are a great way to slow down, and you can only glob onto so much with them in one bite. The balance and artistry of chopsticks takes time and patience, but it is rewarding when you learn something new, and they elevate whatever you are eating with grace and elegance. They make packaged Seven Eleven donuts sexy. Again, please don't eat those.

Until I learned how to use chopsticks, I carried around a set of baby utensils. That was awesome! It worked great especially since I suffer from Dysphagia, or MS related nerve damage affecting the muscles and coordination required for swallowing. It can lead to food or liquids entering the airway instead of the esophagus which can cause choking or lung infections like pneumonia.

Eating quickly or taking large bites, as well as talking or being distracted while chewing, can lead to choking. I vividly recall choking on my salad one night and then coughing up a tiny piece of lettuce straight from my lungs later. We all have our challenges eh? If you want to try carrying around baby utensils, but you want an excuse for anyone watching, say you have an affliction and you need them to prevent choking.

If you find baby utensils or chopsticks unsuitable, practice placing your utensils down and resting your hands in your lap after each bite. Do not pick them up again until you have fully swallowed the previous mouthful. Treat yourself to a special set of adult utensils: one bowl, one plate, one cup. Make them elegant and visually pleasing. If your new dishes are dirty, you'll slow down your eating process by washing them first, which might make you lose your appetite.

A few beautiful dishes at a time found their way into my cupboards. I have a fabulous ramen bowl I bought with my chopsticks at an Asian market. It holds exactly one accurately measured portion; it is handmade, and its beauty inspires me every time I eat from it and other pieces like it. I consistently benefit from predetermined healthy portions, elegantly presented on attractive dishes and my heart smiles.

Don't eat your food standing, ever. Sit down! If you can't sit down and relax to eat then just wait to eat. Wait till you have the time to relax because when you eat standing or doing other things, you are sending unconscious signals to your nervous system to go into fight or flight mode. This keeps cortisol flowing and you unconsciously eat too fast and unfocused. It is the exact opposite of mindfulness. Stop eating while you're doing everything or anything else. Don't drive, walk, talk, work, read, so forth and so on. I would say don't watch tv and eat but I'm also trying to keep it real here.

When out for a romantic dinner with your significant other or a date, you generally don't use your phone at the dinner table right? You don't oversee work emails and the like, it's rude not to give the other person and the romantic night your full attention.

The meal, the restaurant, the time, all represent a value, and it should be respected. Don't forget the actual amount you or the other person spent. Why wouldn't you give yourself the same value and respect? Don't be rude to yourself. Focus on your food and only your food when you're eating. You digest better, get less heartburn and other issues. Love yourself, love your food.

Figure 21: MJ thinking about life in 2017.

Figure 22: MJ thinking about life in 2023, what a difference.

5/3/21   8/17/21

Mind Over Matter, Your Mind Matters

Transcript Audio Journal

"Hardships often prepare ordinary people for an extraordinary destiny."–C.S.Lewis

(commonly attributed but not verified.)

RENEE: I think you asked me what was bothering me. A huge part of my problem was being unable to figure out why I wasn't doing the things I'd been doing so well at for such a long time.

Seriously, I was five pounds away from my lifetime goal weight! Now, feeling out of control again was getting to me more than screwing up in the first place. Suddenly not understanding myself and my relapse was blowing my mind, and I kept looking for things, some reasons why. You know? In our chat with Diana I was missing life on the boat, I told her how much I miss living at the marina and now I'm always stressed and angry. I'm angry with myself.

"It's the anger," she said. "It's because you're angry at yourself and what's going on."

Maybe she's on to something with that. I had all this stress and fear inside while taking care of Dad and wow, so much anger, rage even. It was eating me up inside and do you know what? That's the crux of the issue, it always is. It's always something inside. There's always an outside influence with different degrees of impact, but it's always something inside being bothered that we have to face and deal with. I really want to bring this point home to everyone. Don't ever stop questioning why and question your own why the hardest.

MJ: Maybe Diana's point was also about her own anger. She's been reading "Reinventing Your Life" by Jeffrey Young. She's swearing by this book as a life guide and how it resonated with her so much. You always gotta keep looking for your reasons why, just like we're doing here. You have to get to know yourself really well and be honest about why you do what you do. Be honest but, be fair and kind to yourself.

RENEE: At this point I believe I've found one of my key triggers. Throughout my life, I've struggled with feeling inadequate for the task at hand, any task. I've always felt I have to earn my right to be. Being here in this household has brought up all of those old feelings. I think Imposter Syndrome describes it best.

MJ: You would tell me to be gentle with what you say to yourself.

RENEE: Yeah, there's that…being gentle.

MJ: Didn't you also say it had something to do with having a desire, a desire outside of yourself?

RENEE: Yes! Having an outward-facing desire helps you focus on your goals. It shifts your perspective from self-criticism to self-compassion. When your motivation is tied to a higher purpose, to an external aspiration, it reduces the tendency to dwell on immediate mistakes.

Desire is not necessarily the same thing as your goals either.

MJ: Yeah umm… you can have completely different desires from your goals. Desires are things you want or wish for, like I desire to be wealthy. Goals are specific and come with a plan of action, like if I DESIRE to achieve a GOAL of $10,000.00 in a year, I plan to set aside two hundred dollars each week.

RENEE: A desire can become a goal if you create a concrete plan to achieve it. Your desire needs to always stay strong even though your goals will probably change.

MJ: You still look at me sometimes like, "I don't think you get it." Maybe you just haven't seen the "Aha!" moment on my face yet, but I'll catch a reflection in a window or the mirror or something and I don't recognize myself. I like who I do see though and that's new, it's good and it's important!

I keep going back to my old TikToks you know? It's like I told you the other day, part of me wants to erase the whole damn thing. The other part of me says no you can't because you've got to remember where you came from.

RENEE: Yeah, I would agree wholeheartedly. The work never stops right…

MJ: Exactly, and this new journey into lifting weights is going to be the same way.

RENEE: You're not scrawny by any means, but once you…

MJ: Once I start toning up and start seeing changes, that's gonna be another substitute sugar high.

RENEE: Do you know they've scientifically proven sugar affects us as much as drugs do? Researchers have utilized MRI brain scans to examine individuals experiencing sexual arousal, profound happiness and laughter, as well as the impacts of both drugs and sugar on the brain.

Sugar triggers dopamine release in the same region of our brain associated with addictions to cocaine and heroin. Repeated sugar consumption can lower dopamine levels, making the brain require more sugar to feel the same pleasure, similar to drug tolerance. High-glycemic foods, which quickly convert to sugar in the blood *(such as bread and pasta)*, stimulate significant activity in the brain's pleasure centers similar to joy and laughter. Bread becomes sugar and feels like joy, reinforcing cravings.

This may be why they say laughter is the best medicine. Why do you think people give chocolate away on Valentine's Day? When you wanna get some nooky from your significant other, you give 'em chocolate for the dopamine rush. It's close to good sex and feelings of love. Dopamine baby.

MJ: You're right.

RENEE: It's up to you to choose where you're gonna get your dopamine hit from. Today we got ours from birds.

End of Transcript

Figure 23: Renee & MJ enjoying a Friday night in Ft. Myers 2022.

Figure 24: MJ filled with joy and a sense of accomplishment from climbing the stairs of the Jupiter Lighthouse 2023.

Chapter 8

Crafting Your Own Secret Keys

"The art and science of asking questions is the source of all knowledge." – Thomas Berger

Many people seek a singular solution or key to success. However, it is important to acknowledge there is no single definitive key. I don't believe there is a "one size fits all" in the diet and nutrition world because food is chemistry. Just as we don't always have the same chemistry in the dating world, you may not have proper chemistry for a night on the town with Brussel sprouts or Mac 'N' Cheese while I do.

Nutrigenomics studies how our genes and food interact. Some foods, like broccoli, can affect our genes, turning certain ones on or off to protect our health. Differences in our DNA also change how well we process nutrients like omega-3s or calcium.

By understanding this, we can create diets tailored to our unique genetic needs, improving our health while avoiding universally harmful ingredients. Going forward you may wish to invest in such testing but it's our opinion you can get a good idea based on how you feel after you eat. Journaling is a lot less expensive!

Who remembers when potato chips and other snacks came out with a substance called Olestra marketed by the brand name Olean? It was a synthetic fat meant to be less "fattening," but it caused gastrointestinal issues like diarrhea and cramps for many people. It's not only about what food, but also about what's in the food.

126

(10)In 2003, the FDA removed requirements for labeling transparency concerning Olean/Olestra. One study involving three thousand individuals who did not report adverse effects such as diarrhea overlooked concerns from the Center for Science in the Public Interest. The Center for Science highlighted concerns of potential side effects like fecal incontinence reported by numerous individuals, and the possible increased risks of chronic diseases and cancer due to the obstruction of fat-soluble vitamins such as A, D, E, K, and carotenoids.

It may be beneficial to watch "Food Inc." and other documentaries about the food industry. These sources provide information that might encourage choosing organic, whole foods and grass-fed options. Eating organic, whole foods for a lasting change may mean a different type of budgeting style. It is more expensive, and you need to make it a lifestyle approach fit for your needs.

We didn't always have the ability to shop organically so we made the best choices our wallets and locations could afford. We slowly changed to organics as decent priced options found their way to our shelves. It just worked itself out. Until it does, do the best you can because you're making mindset shifts more permanent than the groceries coming and going.

Maybe this moment isn't the one you totally convert to organic grass-fed everything, but it is the moment you choose a home-made burger wrapped in your favorite lettuce with Dukes Mayo *(it's the only one without sugar we've found carried in most stores)*.

This is the moment you are learning to listen to your body. What is your body doing for you now? Is it making energy for you or is it making you feel fat and uncomfortable? How do you feel and what is the key to feeling better? If I were forced to choose, probably by threat of violence to pick one key, I would say supporting your digestive system and giving yourself holistic nourishment to fight cravings and bad habits. Truly, I would urge everyone to learn about the power and responsibilities of your gut. Study gut health like you're preparing a thesis on the subject. It is called the second brain, and it has A LOT of responsibilities.

As an example, did you know neurotransmitters produced by gut microbes play a critical role in regulating emotions? They produce 95% of the body's serotonin, which regulates mood, appetite, sleep cycles, and pain perception. Your gut is responsible for producing a substance called GABA which calms neural activity reducing feelings of fear and anxiety. Imbalances in your microbes can disrupt neurotransmitters and contribute to depression and other psychiatric disorders. Here's a real kicker, gut microbes make dopamine so I believe keeping our gut as happy and healthy as we possibly can is key.

We should all learn exactly which "health foods" and others to avoid and what it means to be a preservative. A preservative is a substance added to food, cosmetics, and other products to slow down spoilage. Common examples include salt and vinegar which are natural and have their place. Added artificial chemicals are interesting, particularly since our food often shares the same ingredients as our bathroom sundries, our cleaning supplies and um… radiator fluid.

Radiator fluids containing propylene glycol are often marketed as safer alternatives to those with ethylene glycol, because it's less toxic. One example is Prestone LowTox Antifreeze/Coolant, which uses a propylene glycol-based formula. Propylene glycol is commonly found in processed foods as a thickener, stabilizer, or preservative. Examples include salad dressings, cake mixes, frostings, flavored teas, and some ice creams. Yummy, I'll take a sundae with an extra pump of Prestone please…

Also be on the lookout for things like PEG's *(PEG-80)* which can be found in industrial applications, pharmaceuticals, and cosmetics. Basically we're eating from the pharmacy, we're eating our cosmetics, and industrial fluids. I am about to demonstrate to you; we are eating liquid plastic.

In case I failed to mention previously, learning what words on labels mean is important and now you can start by breaking them down by prefix and suffix. Let's practice with PEG. PolyEthylene Glycol is in a lot of our dairy products like generic half and half or whipping cream. Now let's break down the words. POLY- *(means many)* It refers to the fact the compound is made up of many repeating units of Ethylene. Ethylene- A hydrocarbon molecule that comes from crude oil and Glycol- A type of alcohol that makes the compound versatile and soluble in water. Ok, let's put it together and we've got many parts of crude oil mixed with a type of alcohol *(think rubbing alcohol not whiskey)*, so it dissolves in water.

Polyethylene glycol *(PEG)* can be thought of as similar to liquid plastic. While plastics like polyethylene *(used in bags and bottles)* are solid and rigid, PEG is a modified form that remains liquid or semi-solid. It retains some properties like plastic, such as flexibility and chemical stability, but it's designed to be water-soluble and according to the FDA, safe for use in many applications.

129

(11)In 2015 a study was done challenging the FDA's conclusion that PEG's are "safe". In the study, an ELISA test was used. There are many ELISA tests for particular molecules using matching antibodies. This is crazy sciency stuff but, bear with me. ELISA tests are a diagnostic tool used in medicine, biotech fields and plant pathology, among others.

The 2015 study used a high-sensitivity assay for the test and 72% of random blood plasma samples detected PEG antibodies. In layman's speak, high-sensitivity assays are a type of test designed to detect extremely small amounts of a substance in a sample which other tests miss. The samples were collected from 1990 to 1999 meaning it was an obvious health concern decades ago.

Due to its omnipresence in many products it has become unavoidable. With so many people showing antibodies to PEG, it's indicative of an allergic reaction. An allergy to polyethylene glycol *(PEG)* is often identified when a person reacts to various unrelated products like processed foods, cosmetics, medications, or other items containing PEG. Those numbers don't include hypersensitive reactions to PEG. The average person probably has little to no idea what three quarters of the ingredients are in the food and beverages they consume. We are busy, we are pressed, we are stressed.

When I asked MJ to learn about our food labels and decoding ingredient words, I had her make a list and turn it into a 19x27 poster to put in her kitchen. It listed over twenty-five different names used to disguise sugar in our food and drink. I told her, "When you stare at this list of words, they will start to become familiar to you.

You'll be reminded daily the word maltodextrin is a particularly hellish nightmare version of sugar for your insulin and hormone levels."

Nobody has time to give a spit what maltodextrin is. Keep it simple, put a poster in your face if you're old school and love laminating stuff like I do, or you can just get yourself an app for your phone. Look up one called Trash Panda. It flags potentially harmful ingredients in food, and offers scientific research on flagged items as well as allowing you to create personalized shopping lists.

Hopefully, you will become passionate enough to dig deep. Maybe you'll begin to see different ads in which companies are taking advantage of us through loopholes in the rules of the FDA *(and there are a lot)*. An incredibly concerning example is the (12)**GRAS loophole.** This acronym stands for "Generally Recognized As Safe."

Manufacturers can self-certify ingredients as GRAS without FDA oversight since 1958, allowing potentially harmful substances into foods. The more people who become deeply invested in protecting our food chain and change their buying habits, the greater our collective purchasing power becomes. This unified effort forces corporations to pay attention to our demand for clean, healthy, and responsibly sourced food.

Back to things we can do at home, we need to start adding nature's fat loss helpers. Nature has provided us with many plants, vitamins, minerals and other remarkable stuff to actually help you get away with eating foods that aren't great for you. When you do have a Prestone Low-Tox flavored ice cream, you need to help your body eliminate toxins while turning the fat into energy.

Adding things like vitamins and minerals to your daily or weekly regimen can help mitigate ill-effects of bad decisions or poor conditions. Enzymes such as lipase, amylase and bromelain aid in digestion, assist with metabolism and function as anti-inflammatories. For you pineapple lovers out there think Bromelain.

Start at the source with most problems. A lot of our weight issues are due to our digestive system. It processes food and produces energy for our body, mind, and spirit. If digestion is impaired, everything else suffers. You need probiotics and prebiotics, but don't go out and spend money on a bunch of probiotics from the bargain bin at your local drug store, no don't do that. Probiotics have to survive your stomach acid and have to be quality, LIPOSOMAL supplements. Practically all supplements should be liposomal to survive your stomach acid.

Many experts recommend probiotics with at least ten billion CFUs per serving to ensure enough beneficial bacteria reach your gut. CFU stands for Colony Forming Units. However, the ideal CFU count can vary depending on individual needs and the specific health benefits you're seeking.

The effectiveness of a probiotic depends more on which bacteria it contains and not so much on how many different kinds of bacteria. Caralluma Fimbriata can help fight cravings with their appetite-suppressing properties and its use in weight management supplements can help with your discipline.

The food we eat today is not the same food of our ancestors, it's not even the same food of our great grandparents and when I say food I'm talking about a loaf of bread. Our food is changing, and not necessarily for the better. We grow, handle, harvest, process, prepare, and consume food in ways that our bodies do not recognize. As a result, when our bodies can't process these foods, they store them as fat.

Have you ever added salt to a pot of boiling water? When I make pasta I put the olive oil and salt in the water as I set it to boil, and if you'll notice, the oil floating on top of the water travels around the pot, grabbing the salt particles where it holds it until a rolling boil starts. When the rolling boil starts, and the little oil islands start to break up from all of the action, the salt is released into the water to melt.

My point is this, our body fat also takes protective measures. Imagine your self-storage locker full of all the crap you don't know what to do with, some of it like old tool blades or saws could be dangerous if we left them scattered about our homes. Our body fat grabs and holds substances it doesn't recognize or cannot process such as toxins to protect vital organs from potential harm.

What happens when you run out of space in the closet sized mini locker you rented? You either dump some stuff or rent another locker right? Well, detox your body, dump some weight or open up more fat storage units and get bigger.

It all gets stored in our adipose tissue until we metabolize the fat. As we burn fat based on energy needs, those substances may be released into the bloodstream if they can't be metabolized. Your kidneys and liver have to detoxify your blood, and you excrete it. This is also why drinking water is so important. Like in the pot, when the fat finally releases the particles, it dissolves in the water. We need to drink plenty of water to assist in moving the good stuff around and to help pee out the bad stuff.

EGCG *(Epigallocatechin gallate)* is a naturally occurring, plant based, compound, and evidence suggests it can reduce inflammation, help you lose weight and suppress appetite as well as help fight off brain disorders and heart disease. EGCG is the main health benefit attributed to green tea as well as smaller amounts in other teas such as white tea, oolong, and black teas.

EGCG is present to a lesser degree in other plant-based foods that haven't been studied as well. I recommend cranberries, blueberries and blackberries. Fruits have polyphenols and flavonoids. They do, however, come with their naturally occurring fructose *(A.K.A. sugar)* and we're going to leave the majority of fruits alone for a hot minute anyway.

Nuts, red wine and legumes can be a source of these helpers if you keep in mind they are highly inflammatory with auto immune disorders. For anyone living with MS or even other inflammatory and auto immune diseases, I recommend books by Dr. Terry Wahls titled "The Wahls Protocol" and "Minding My Mitochondria."

To our delight and yours, these phytonutrients can also be found in avocados and dark chocolate of at least seventy percent cacao. Don't expect it to taste like Hersey's Kisses though, and if you can get all of these benefits from having a spot of tea too, well why wouldn't you right? What time is it where you are? Is it teatime? Maybe you should take a wee break to make some tea and bring it back here for another tiny science break? Seriously, go make some tea and I'll wait…

TINY SCIENCE BREAK

Many diseases and disorders can originate in the mouth if proper care of gums and teeth, such as regular flossing, is not maintained.

Rumor has it, flossing every day adds six years to your life. There's another argument stating flossing is not a good idea but, you should try "pulling" with oil. All camps agree on the importance of good oral care and suggest using a combination of the two. Be sure to check the ingredients of your floss.

Our teeth and mouth are also the very beginning of digestion. As we chew our food, we break it down into usable pieces and it mixes with saliva which has digestive enzymes. Our spit is actually very powerful and amazing. Just in case you have never fully appreciated your spit, here is a list of things your spit does in your mouth: Defends against invaders such as bad microbes, defends you against bad decisions like licking nail polish from your fingers to test for dryness. It defends you against mechanical injuries *(I'll leave that to your imagination)*, and the list goes on.

It heals the inside of your cheek when you chew a hole in your face and restores other soft tissue damage, it keeps your mouth lubricated and a lubricated mouth is good for many things. Have you ever tried kissing with a dry mouth? It's not fun and a dry mouth makes it easier to pass infection along. Saliva not only digests but also fights germs. It contains phosphate, bicarbonate, and protein buffers that help maintain a proper pH range in the mouth. I'm going to keep saying mouth, it sounds prettier than things like oral cavity.

When you put something in your mouth, the flow of spit increases according to the taste. YEP! Even our taste buds play an important role, and our tongues are often smarter than us when used for things other than speaking. The flow of saliva not only changes according to the taste but also the concentration and consistency of whatever is in our oral cavity. When the flow of saliva increases, a swallowing reflex is triggered.

Keep in mind I'm trying to be quick and easy here. I am calling this a "tiny" science break so I must oversimplify things a tad. Anyway, as I was saying, our saliva contains salivary amylase as well, to help pancreatic amylase break down complex carbohydrates into simple sugars. Your spit contains Lipase *(also as an aid to your gastric and pancreatic lipase)* to start digesting fats into fatty acids and now, your small intestines can absorb those fatty acids and sugars.

It makes sense to me that if I'm deficient in these enzymes, to take them as supplements for maintaining optimum health, diet and weight. Before I break from tiny science break, lets segue over to the C word. Let's talk a bit more about carbohydrates.

We've got complex carbs and simple carbs like sweet potatoes or yams. Potatoes, rice, bread and pasta are technically complex but, less fibrous with more starch. Simple sugar is like getting an IV bag of Kool-Aid. It's easy to see how syrup, sugar, fructose, corn syrup, and high fructose corn syrup go straight in like a heroin needle.

Consider your carb intake according to how much fiber it is likely to have. When you open up a yam or a sweet potato you can actually see the fiber content, all those little stringy things dangling from your fork. Potatoes will clump a bit and sit up on your fork as well as rice but it's starch more than fiber.

As your body digests food and moves it through your intestines, it extracts, sorts, and uses the nutrients it needs. Foods high in soluble fiber slow down this digestive process, causing carbohydrates to travel further along your digestive tract before sugars like glucose, fructose, lactose, and maltose can be absorbed. Since your body can't break down fiber, it passes through your system, carrying some sugars with it. This means sugars, anything ending in "ose" —get trapped and delayed by the fiber, taking longer to be absorbed into your bloodstream and resulting in a slower rise in blood sugar levels.

This folks is why fiber is so important. Iceberg lettuce is more of a hydrating roughage than fiber, but it has another duty, *(Ha! Pun intended for sure!)* as a janitor for scrubbing toxic slime off your intestinal walls which prevents absorption of nutrients. If you've heard the words slow carbs and low carbs, this is where it all makes sense. A slow carb is a complex carb *(having lots of fiber)* which slowly breaks down into your blood through your intestinal walls and does not cause a sharp increase in blood sugar or corresponding insulin levels, unlike simple sugars or refined carbs which are absorbed directly.

Every time you put things in your mouth it sends signals to the brain. We make the motions of chewing, mixing, and squeezing with our mouths and tongues and this activity signals the rest of our systems to get busy doing all the things necessary for proper digestion. So, take good care of your teeth for the proper chewing and break down of your food.

We started this conversation at the beginning of digestion and let's end at the bottom, shall we? Let's talk about the pooper and what comes out of it. Do you know what comes out of it, in detail? If you really care about good health and changing it, then it's time to turn around and start looking at your remains of the day.

Our poop tells us many things about what is going on inside. For example, if your body isn't producing enough lipase *(a digestive enzyme)*

137

your poop is likely to be greasy or sticky. Think of Dawn dish detergent cutting the bacon grease clean off your pans. These digestive enzymes are delivered straight to the gut tube via little ducts whereas hormones, which also have a huge impact on digestion, are delivered straight to your bloodstream for other digestion processes.

Interestingly enough, Dawn and other detergents are made with enzymes from the same protein digesting family called Protease. Notice how *p r o t* e are the first letters in the word protein and protease? This is not an accident. Let's break down the words. The prefix prote- in both words originate from Greek meaning first or primary importance.

Proteins were named to reflect their essential role in life processes as they are fundamental building blocks of living organisms and Proteases are enzymes specifically meant to break them down. You can retain a lot of helpful information by learning how to break down complicated words into their simple components and memorizing what they do. I bet you haven't forgotten what 'ose' represents or PEG either. As you learn to read ingredients list, you start to digest all those crazy words along with your food.

There are many compounds we humans need for optimal performance and treatment or prevention of chronic diseases. According to an increasing number of studies, compounds called phytochemicals *(Phyto- Greek for plant)* are a biggie and very beneficial to us humans. The largest variety of these plant chemicals are called polyphenols *(poly=many + phenol=organic, acidic compound with antiseptic properties such as Listerine)*. There are many different groups of compounds in the polyphenols and one group are called tannins. One of the legs under the title of tannins are the catechins.

138

Catechins are specific tannins making up eighty-five percent of the tannins found in tea as we've mentioned. All tannins are a broad group of poly phenol compounds possessing antioxidant properties. Another leg beneath the title of tannins is tannic acid, a brown and bitter organic compound predominantly found in the tissues of woody, flowering plants such as bark and nuts. It has been shown to potentially reduce total cholesterol levels and blood pressure, as well as stimulate the immune system. The order these follow can be a tad confusing, so I have attempted to summarize the breakdown in a one-line flow chart. *(Phytochemicals→Polyphenols→Tannin→Catechins→Antioxidants).*

In the tannin family is where we find EGCG. The compound EGCG Epigallocatechin-3-0-Gallate is a condensed tannin from green tea leaves that evidently inhibits strokes and increases the lifespan of lab rats. May we remind you, however, this is green tea WITHOUT SUGAR or sweetener of any kind.

These compounds work as powerful antioxidants. Surely you all know about antioxidants by now and how they help repair and protect against cellular damage? Look it up if you don't know. They're in berries as well as legumes and nuts.

In summation, the beginning of your digestive system is your mouth and how you chew. The health of your mouth, teeth, and gums are VITAL and almost never addressed by our physicians who don't specialize in the mouth. Our medical system typically treats health issues in isolation rather than as part of an interconnected whole. It's essential to consider the entire system, as one part affects another. Anyway, I digress….**End of not so Tiny Science Break**

Figure 25: Renee & MJ enroute to Machu Picchu via Inca Rail.

Oh what an adventure!

Figure 26: MJ standing against a wall on Tandapata in Cusco Peru. According to MJ the Peru adventure was life-changing.

Chapter 9
Wrapped Up for Take Out: Your Summary

"Whether you make one or all of these changes, you are making changes - and everything counts. What you do today will change the way you feel about tomorrow. The way you feel today and tomorrow could change how you feel next week. The choice is yours." – R. Ganzel

A Chicken Caesar Wrap with house-made Caesar dressing sounds delicious. Consider using egg or cheese wraps instead of flour. They also make rice paper wraps for vegans. As for the carbohydrate situation with rice, there's a little-known fact about cold rice, cold starch actually. It helps stabilize blood sugar and insulin spikes which, if you've been paying attention at all, you know is also KEY. I do recommend deeper research if you wish to keep resistant starch in your diet as not all resistant starches are created equal and there are a lot of caveats, clauses and fine print involved.

I would like to leave you with a clear breakdown. What are we putting in your take-out box? Let's start with a fortune cookie, *Every step is a step so just keep stepping one step at a time.* My fortune cookies always had simple, stupid, universal truths. Keep stepping up to your own situation, keep stepping towards things that grab you and move you. If this book encourages you to take a more proactive approach to your health, treatments, or comprehension of your body's functions, we will consider it a success.

What can you do now, what's next? Go forth and lean HARD into anything and everything that works for you as an individual. Watch videos or just listen to them as you brush your teeth, over coffee or in the car. Pick a regularly scheduled time in the day for an hour devoted to research about your health issues and other studies. Take note of things that impress you or work for you.

Park at the back of every parking lot every time, walk up a few flights of stairs before getting on an elevator. Every week you will find yourself walking more and more flights and longer distances. Try sitting on a yoga ball at your desk at work. They make chairs out of yoga balls too, complete with wheels to spin around.

You can even add onto this by adding weights to your arms and/or legs. Now, basic data entry and phone calls become a workout as well as a trip to the copy machines and break room. If you're a domestic god/goddess, then laundry room trips and folding are a workout with added challenge!

DRINK WATER. Have I mentioned water in this book yet? DRINK WATER. Take matters into your own hands and drink more water. Feeling hungry, drink water. Feeling peckish, drink water. Want to smack your co-worker right across the mouth, go to the water cooler with your wrist and ankle weights on and drink some water.

Order your own lab tests, including genetic testing, and create a personal medical file as you can afford them. Learn all about yourself, spend time with your body. I'll never forget the look of shock and awe on my general practioner's face when I went to him for this tiny, almost imperceptible bump in my neck. He couldn't find it at first and I had to help him. When he finally felt the bump, he was so surprised,

"Boy, you really are in touch with your body, aren't you?" He said while shaking his head in a befuddled fashion. LEARN YOUR BODY WELL.

Eat a pound of veggies every day and learn what veggies actually are and are not. Eat a rainbow a day by eating as many colors in your food as you can. I find salads to be the most effective way to do this. Salads by their nature put rainbows on your plate. For example, red is in radishes, because for me tomatoes, peppers, and anything else in the nightshade family are very inflammatory.

Orange can come from carrots, peppers, heirloom tomatoes, and an orange with your salad. It should be the whole orange though or a part of it. Don't juice it or drink it. You need the fibers in the orange to moderate the sugar content and control insulin responses.

This is true with all your food, fruits and almost anything. Don't tear down and eat your foods in a de-natured state. *(Unnatural state.)* Again, chemistry... remember our high school chemistry labs? How about when you try to bake without certain ingredients? Things go really wrong, don't they? Even sugar is better before it's processed so if you must have it at all go for sugar in the raw.

Eating egg whites without the yolk makes a chemical mess. The yolk contains fat-soluble vitamins *(A, D, E, and K)* and other components the body needs to absorb and utilize the protein and nutrients in the egg white effectively. Without these, your body may struggle to process the protein efficiently, leading to potential metabolic or digestive challenges over time. So, eating the whole egg provides a more complete nutrient profile.

If you're limiting yolks for any reason, it's essential to ensure you're still getting the nutrients they offer from other food sources. Also, eggs are yellow. They're orange if you get the good eggs which I hope by now I've convinced you to accept nothing other than organic, VEGETARIAN FED eggs. Yellow can also come from summer squash, bell peppers *(again unless you have an autoimmune disorder or any inflammatory issues.)*

Green comes with many different leaves. My favorite is arugula which also happens to be one of the healthiest options. Spring mix gives you more reds and purple with radicchio leaves or swiss chard. You should avoid raw spinach though. Remember, chemistry? Iceberg lettuce offers mainly fiber, water, and roughage with little nutritional value. Romaine is decent. Green is an easy one.

Blue is available in blueberries. Berries are a bit different than fruit and I get a little resentful when they are lumped into the same category as all other fruits. When you eat fruit, try to stay with the darker fruits like purple plums, concord, or black grapes and cherries. The darker the fruit or berry, the less sugar it has making the berry family an excellent choice. You've just eaten a rainbow all in one bowl and if it equaled a pound without your salad dressing, congratulations!

We are suggesting you pay attention, pay attention to what is working and what is not, what is making you feel better and what is getting results. We are suggesting you be open to change and experiment frequently with guidance from your health care team, to do research and find a medical team willing to work with YOU as a team for YOUR health.

Although meticulous care has been taken in proofreading and editing for content accuracy and research validity, we acknowledge that we are human and can only share our personal experiences with you. As I've stated multiple times, I am NOT a doctor, I have no formal medical training or certifications, and I do not advise anyone on their conditions or how to treat them.

I have, however, tried to learn from people who are doctors and followed their advice with a lot of great successes. The doctors I recommend are listed in our book as additional resources. They have extensive research material that is sensible and verifiable. Having said, please enjoy the list of links, sources, videos etc. that we will leave here for you at the back of the book.

Figure 27: This is special to both of us, this was a daily ritual for us on Idle Time, Renee's boat in Ft Myers Florida.

Love Offerings

Transcripts Audio Journal

"Life is the flower for which love is the honey." – Victor Hugo

RENEE: What are some things we do when we feel passion?

MJ: The first thing I think of is making love.

RENEE: And you're not alone. Odds are most people would say the same thing off the top of their heads. However, the phrase isn't making sex it's making love. Think about it, you're in the kitchen making a wonderful meal using good food which is a good life and so you're giving good food and good life and that's a love offering. You are literally in the kitchen making love to yourself and anyone else you plan on feeding.

MJ: Okay, I'm following this, keep going.

RENEE: Passion involves experiencing your food with all your senses, which adds a sexual component. For further research, brain scans have been used to predict eating and sexual behavior. These studies highlight the interconnected nature of brain responses to food and sex while also emphasizing gender-specific differences.

MJ: Dopamine?

RENEE: You know it!

MJ: So savor the moment, the tastes, and the smells. You know, everyone knows what it's like to open a package of chicken breast and put it on the cutting board.

RENEE: Does it remind you of anything else when you hold it in your hand? You are stimulating your imagination and creating new and passionate connections in your brain. Again, it's the whole life approach in a passionate mindset.

MJ: I totally agree.

RENEE: If you enjoy horror movies and food, I recommend watching "The Menu" for its appreciation of the culinary arts. If it wasn't actually a horror movie, I would have called it an inspirational flick. The narrative centers on an exclusive evening at a high-end restaurant, where patrons are treated to a sequence of exceptional dishes expertly prepared by a renowned chef.

Many times I felt a bit envious of several lines the characters used to describe food and their relationships with it. My favorite line went something like,

(13)**CHEF:** **"I do not want you to eat. I want you to taste, to savor..."** This attitude is primo. It represents top quality in food relationships and is of utmost importance.

MJ: I don't think my life really started until we met, and I got on your plan. My head space wasn't the greatest, but when we started talking about your plan you made it sound so easy.

Three months into sharing your nutritional information with me by messenger, we started doing video chats. For two of those months, I primarily drank water despite having the option to include tea. The taste of plain tea without sugar was not appealing. It wasn't until I got down here, I actually was able to accept the tea with no sugar at all. That's also when I lost another seventy-four pounds. So, eliminating sugar from my diet was the ultimate key, but you made it easy. You made it attainable. You didn't say,

"Alright, quit sugar cold turkey." That would be like quitting smoking cold turkey. It's hard to do! It all comes down to you coach. You gave me tools to help me help myself and you helped me with the baby steps along the way.

I have a hardness about me, and I do things the hard way. I think I was pretty committed, but I also think somebody who didn't have a stubborn streak might have been able to attain their goals even quicker.

RENEE: I don't know, I feel like your stubbornness helped you on this path because you're oriented towards thoughts such as, "I'll do this no matter what!" How would you say I made it easy? Can you remember any particular instance in which you had a task or something you needed to commit to where you went, "Oh crap! This is easier than I thought?"

MJ: Yeah, I did actually. I went to the beach and walked past the pole. I walked for three miles and came back three miles. I didn't realize how easy it would be or how fast I would be able to start walking distances.

In the first two weeks, I walked a quarter of a mile to the pole. I increased to a two-mile walk a week later and, within a few weeks, I progressed to walking six miles. Then one day I decided I'm gonna walk all the way to the crab shack.

RENEE: That was a nine-mile walk, and for a second time I was pissed at you after the fact. It was too much at once and with your particular foot and ankle situation, it made me feel scared. I thought I had better explained how crucial it is to pay attention to your body's signals, especially since we weren't at the same location. Paying close attention and listening to our bodies is a huge, key element.

MJ: Yes, concentrate on what you're getting ready to consider putting in your mouth and that honestly was a game changer for me. Here I was for the first time, pulling up to a drive through window and saying to myself, "Let's not take a #4 super-size and you know what, let's not go ahead and get an extra sandwich."

RENEE: That's awesome!

MJ: And you know, not just shove it in your mouth like Homer Simpson. I couldn't do it, you know? I wasn't the same in that moment. Maybe because I felt connected with my food after everything, after I gave it so much mental work, thought and preparation.

RENEE: Yes! Get connected with your food!

MJ: It's rewarding to eat and to prep meals the way you requested. It makes me want to savor my lunch hour. I know a week or so ago, you got on to me because I engulfed my food.

RENEE: Oh, when I made eggs with asparagus.

MJ: I thought, what the heck, it's protein you know. It's just egg and asparagus for breakfast and not a large portion, did I really need to be slow and thoughtful with something this small?

RENEE: Yes! Yes, you do, if you bite it, consider it.

MJ: And it's because of learning to enjoy the task of creating and preparing my foods I've gotten to this point. I appreciate my food in ways I never thought of before. I appreciate what I'm putting in my body and learning "I am what I eat." The way you took notes on different things and shared them with me, I would hear your voice telling me to stay away from these things I loved, like bell peppers. I knew they were bad for my arthritis, and it would be best to eliminate or at least really limit them from what I eat.

RENEE: You can still have flavor bursts of bell peppers and tomatoes in your mouth occasionally without making it an everyday part of your life.

MJ: Yes, and by taking them out and replacing them with new things full of great flavor my palate grew. Now I'm experiencing all kinds of new things. I'm more open to new ideas and this seems to be spreading to all areas of my life. Eating healthy food has changed me for the better as a whole person and the food tastes better than a #4 super-size any day!

RENEE: Yes, moments like these are so exciting for me!

MJ: You've done something nobody else had. You gave me options. You didn't give me a black and white answer, and you never said you gotta do this or you're doomed.

RENEE: So, for you, personal attention to your specific details as well as support and options tailored for you personally were all key ingredients?

MJ: Yes, exactly. Do you know there was never in my life a mention of eating a pound of vegetables a day? Back when I first started with you and you told me how important it is to eat a pound of veggies a day, I was looking at this package of vegetables *(frozen vegetables even)* and I'm like, "Alright, well this seems like a lot."

RENEE: You didn't fully get with me on this at first. You thought I was crazy I know.

MJ: Really! I mean, how could it be any different than eating several fistfuls of Colt's Pig Stand Barbecue drowned in more sauce than meat? These are the kinds of things I would think to myself. What's the difference?

Well, now I understand. The difference is in ingredients and also in how things are prepared. Barbecue sauce is gonna have some kind of sugar in it regardless of what name it goes under. Sugary protein, that's a no-no you've taught me. Do I miss it? Yeah, I miss it, but you know that little place downtown where we get the General Tso's cauliflower?

RENEE: Yeah, the cauliflower is a replacement for the noodles and without the chicken you're not mixing proteins and sugar. Plus, cauliflower is so amazing for us.

MJ: I know it's not something we could have every day because obviously the sauce has a lot of sweetener in it.

RENEE: We shouldn't eat out too frequently anyway, regardless of what we order. We have little control or knowledge about how our food is handled or prepared. As you become accustomed to reviewing the ingredients list of each and every product you put in your food, you realize the difficulty in finding items that do not contain sugar. Many products contain substantial quantities of sugar.

If consumers encounter difficulties in purchasing organic and sugar-free items for home use, it is likely that restaurants experience similar challenges and don't prioritize these options. Every time you eat out, nine out of ten times you are going to eat an excessive amount of sugar no matter what you choose from the menu.

MJ: I think it's a mindset. Once you start seeing a little bit of success, and I'm pretty sure my friend can agree, you know she lost some weight within the first two weeks...

RENEE: Are you talking about the friend of yours from school? The one I worked with for a couple of weeks?

MJ: Yeah, she lost fifteen pounds. When the tools become yours and you have the support system, which I do now with you, it's a lot easier to change your mindset.

It's like you said, you have to have the desire. Once you identify the desire, you have to grow the determination to make the right decisions and when you show your determination, there will be somebody, something, somewhere and the tools to help you make the right decisions. That kind of support goes a long way. It does something for you. It'll give you an ego boost and that's pretty much what happened for me.

At one point I was getting discouraged because I got stuck in this two hundred and forty to two hundred and forty-eight-pound range...

RENEE: Are you talking about when we were trying to get you down to the maximum weight limit for skydiving?

MJ: Yes. It was an easy solution because you monitored my diet closely when I got here. You showed me where I was derailing myself without realizing it and you also got me walking again.

RENEE: And the sleep patterns!

MJ: Wow! Yeah, the sleep alone because you're right, when I was in Ormond, even though I would go for a good walk I was still coming home and sitting around in the house. I'd get bored or tired or whatever and end up taking a nap, so I struggled to get a good night's rest.

RENEE: I'm sure there was more to your sleep issues, there usually is. Nevertheless, we had to break the habit because it certainly wasn't helping.

MJ: And I did. While going through my TikTok videos I noticed the whole change in my face too. That's when I knew for sure it was working. I realized it had been working before, it just wasn't working as fast, and I can sit here and honestly say now I know why. Even though I was committed and giving my all physically and dietary-wise, I was still missing certain key elements. I think sleep was a big one.

We'd wake up at seven am, be out the door by seven-thirty for a walk. We'd get off the phone and you'd do your thing. I'd usually go out to the shop and start screwing around out there until I got tired and hungry around eleven or eleven-thirty. I would get super munchy always at night. So, I started going for another walk and making TikTok videos.

RENEE: Hold on, sorry continue, keep your voice up for the recording.

MJ: I realized my fat was starting to slide off like butter. I love my sister. I love my family but, they all have poor eating habits. It's like being an ex-smoker and walking into a smoke-filled bar. It felt the same way with trying to eat right. There were times I would go into the kitchen and MY fridge where I kept the organic chicken, and the veggies would be gone!

RENEE: I was getting ready to have you go get a refrigerator for your room because that was frustrating me.

MJ: I'd get so frustrated as well and it would put a whole wrench in my meal plan. I'd have to re-plan and go buy everything all over again.

RENEE: Family and friends can sometimes undermine your efforts, which is why I've discussed support issues. I'm also gonna put the possible need for a mini fridge in here.

MJ: They call me to say they're stopping at Wendy's; do I want a burger? No! I mean thanks for the thought but, no. It's definitely a difference having a supportive team behind you. I can remember one time we all went to Universal and for the first time ever, I had Butterbeer. I knew it was full of sugar. Everyone was like, "Oh, come on! it's just a little bit, you don't even have to drink the whole thing."

It was something so sickly sweet but, then you know my taste buds were changing.

RENEE: It's amazing how fast your taste buds changed, huh?

MJ: Yeah, but they weren't doing it to sabotage me, they were doing it because they knew I've never had it and they wanted me to enjoy the same pleasure as them. Finally I was like fine, yeah and then I drank half of it. After, I asked myself why did I drink that? Somehow I didn't know I could take one sip and be like, there, I tried it, you're right this is good but, it's not good for me. Maybe inside we just don't know we can say no.

RENEE: That's what I think you did well. You didn't down the whole thing. Halfway through, you realized this isn't working and you stopped. You are allowed to change your mind.

MJ: Now the one thing I know I have to really watch myself with, and this was definitely a problem in Ormond, is alcoholic beverages. I come back to the mental part of it, you know I was doing the mental work myself but, alcohol is my go-to. Hiding in the bottle felt harder for me to break than smoking honestly.

RENEE: I think alcohol is hard for everyone.

MJ: It's still hard for me today you know. The beer wasn't doing it for me. I had to go a little harder so it would knock me out, put me to sleep and I love Fireball and all that sugar. I think you put up with it for like, two times before you said anything.

"Listen, we're doing all this amazing work," you said, "and you drink one shot of that stuff and then we have to start over." I think it was then I put my mind to it, you're either online or not. So, no longer would I be indulging until you approved of any alcoholic drinks.

You said quit drinking the mixers and stuff, start with something low carb. You gave me a list, and I picked the best one. Now does it mean I can go out and drink six of them? Do these alternative drinks mean I can go to the bar 2-3 times a week? Yes, but I need to be prepared for the next morning when I jump up on the scale. It's an awareness thing for me now, because of tools you gave me.

RENEE: Frequently, it's an awareness thing. You know, just being made aware of behaviors, being aware of options, like the option of

156

saying no for example. Or being made aware of the fact you were killing days of effort in a single shot. Literally.

MJ: I wanna say something about failure and what I have learned through the years. I've heard I was a screw up my whole life *(that may not be what was said but, that's what I heard)* and it's far from the truth, I know this. I think people should look at it as you don't fail if you're learning; you're actually succeeding.

RENEE: Yes! When you're presented with the issue and you accept the word "fail" you're not failing, you're giving up. I saw this in a quote somewhere, by the way.

MJ: If you fail at something and you keep trying, eventually like these small habits, you're gonna see you have all the tools so it's up to you. Take yesterday for example; I hadn't eaten all day. I was prepared not to until you were ready, but I had so much time between then and the last time I ate, my body stopped wanting to I realized. So I think it gets to a point where you're not so food centric.

RENEE: Yeah you just eat to live instead of living to eat.

MJ: We can be somewhere, like at the fair the other night, all those old, familiar smells like deep fried Oreos. I could get fat just walking through there and we still had an elephant ear puff pastry with cinnamon and sugar.

RENEE: So much grease and fried dough, and you still woke up one pound smaller the next day so there's definitely a science to it.

MJ: Listen, check with your doctors and be prepared for them to tell you you're crazy and then when they start seeing results, be prepared for them to tell you,

"Whatever she's telling you keep on doing it."

RENEE: That happened with your doctors?

MJ: It did. My doctor said to me during a follow up visit,
"I'm not supposed to tell you this and I don't know what she's got you doing, but keep on going."

RENEE: OK so take me back… we were just talking about small habits versus your mind.

MJ: When you go grocery shopping, you say no to the naughty list once, right?

RENEE: While you're at the store you only have to say no once and then don't bring it home. Now you don't have to continually say no every time you remember it's there.

MJ: Whenever I go to stores, I have a habit of bringing home shit. I'll go to seven-eleven to pick up something, lottery tickets, whatever and I'll bring you home something on the no-no list because I think, "Oh well, she deserves a treat" and I bring it home and you're like… "DAMN IT MJ!" I got it now. I understand I just put you in a bad position again. Not only are you saying no to opening the package at all but, if it's a package of twenty-five pieces, you're saying no to it twenty-five times. You're also having to say no to me. There's gotta be some guilt there too right? You know I was trying to show you love and saying no is saying no to me as well.

RENEE: Yeah, we did good though.

MJ: We did! And I don't know if you noticed, but we went for sixteen hours without eating. We went back to our sixteen-hour intermittent fasting mark today and we did good with our carbs, sugars, and portions.

RENEE: We only had a little bit. I had the wrap on my chimichanga, so I didn't do perfectly, but you know, baby steps back to our own program here.

MJ: Exactly! And we did good. We did sixteen hours; we didn't eat until the time we set. We did more than sixteen hours actually, more like twenty and most of our meal was protein and fats.

RENEE: Yeah, the only carbs we really had were the corn tortilla chips, and I had a Margarita. I did choose the skinny one without all the sugary mix. It was Don Julio with lime, lemon, and salt, and then we get home and what do I do, I grab a handful of jellybeans.

Granted it was a small handful, and I didn't lay down with it. Had they not been here, I wouldn't have had to keep telling myself no so that's a thing.

MJ: Tiny habits. So, if you're at the grocery store, hold on. You can say no for the two minutes it takes to get to the end of the aisle or to skip it all together.

RENEE: Precisely. You can resist for ten minutes while you shop for other things, keep saying no to the bad habits for another twenty minutes while you wait in line and unload for the cashier. You can do it for thirty minutes while everything gets packed away and out to the car. You can do it for forty minutes as you finish your expedition and head home. You can do these things for one hour of your life at a time, things that seem impossible for a lifetime.

Think about it in these terms because when you think about all of this in terms of forever, you could easily be overwhelmed.

MJ: And if you still want whatever "it" was so badly, you end up raiding the pantry looking for anything to kill the urge?

RENEE: You should take a walk, preferably over driving, to the nearest convenience store and buy ONE serving of the "it" you are craving. Not a bag of them, not a shareable size, just a standard, single serving, and take it home.

MJ: If you're at the grocery store and you walk through the candy aisle, you know what you're doing? You're talking to yourself and being your own coach.

RENEE: Or you actually get on the phone or video with your coach or a "sponsor" or mentor to walk you through your grocery trips in the beginning. Talk. Talk and walk, that's right, just keep walking, and talking. Even if it has to be talking out loud to yourself and you're like... "That's it! You're doing so good, just keep on walking. No not today Satan not today."

MJ: You walk out of the grocery store, you go home, you unload your groceries and do your cooking or whatever. You have your dinner and then, oh damn, you know, I'd really like those sweets now. Guess what? Too bad. You don't have any and you're at your weakest moment, which is usually right after dinner or just because it's in the evening and it soothes you.

RENEE: If it's not there you can be weak all you want so you just don't bring it home with you. I'm not telling you no, I'm telling you yes but in a different way. I'm saying "wait." So instead of bringing home a bag of jellybeans and a six pack of king size Reese's cups, I'm telling you leave them in the grocery store.

If you still want it after dinner and are willing to put your shoes back on, go out, and return to the nearest convenience store to get it, then feel free to do so. Hopefully, you don't live right next door.

MJ: What if you do live next door to the Seven Eleven but you're in Butte Montana and it's six degrees below zero?

RENEE: OK well, now you have more choices. How bad do you want it? Do you want it bad enough to put your parka back on and go out in the snow for it? Maybe your snow boots are wet, and you have to get your tired but off your couch, go down a flight of stairs and stumble to the Seven Eleven across the street for those Reese's. Guess what? You are gonna have to really want the candy at this point!

MJ: Maybe I'd even go down three flights of stairs because I live in an apartment building?

RENEE: Even better! If you do decide to go get those Reese's cups, give yourself some slack and just walk all the stairs to help offset the negative impact of sweets. This isn't torture. Nobody wants a third job trying to lose weight.

The idea is to make the lesser choice as inconvenient as possible and the better choice the most convenient. If you really want those Reese's peanut butter cups and you're willing to put the boots and the parka back on, go ahead.

MJ: And maybe you misplaced your keys? Now, when you think "Oh, I'm going back out for a snack, where's my keys? Damn it, now I gotta sit here and look for them."

RENEE: Who knows, maybe by the time it's all figured out, you'll lose interest in those Reese's peanut butter cups because you had to go through so much. And if you don't, you still gotta walk down the stairs even if you do at least one flight and hop on the elevator. You will do two flights next week.

161

If you live two blocks from the Seven Eleven don't ride, walk, walk, walk. When you buy the Reese's peanut butter cups, don't buy the king size with four of them in there. You buy the one-serving size with two peanut butter cups, and you eat them on the walk home, again, you're compensating for the excess sugar, particularly if it's after dark.

This way you've started the process of mobilizing the sugar through your bloodstream instead of bringing it back home to sit on the couch with you.

BREAK FOR STAFF MEETING (*A.K.A. bathroom break*)

MJ: I like what you were just saying about how you taught me to respect food, we've lost that.

RENEE: People have gotten to the point where we don't even see food as food anymore, it's a package, it's a box, it's a pouch, it's a cellophane wrapper. It's three minutes in the microwave. It's a number two; it's a number six super-sized.

MJ: You make some pretty good points. It's the same way we've dehumanized so much of our life. We've depersonalized our food, and you forget what it's supposed to do for you.

RENEE: Exactly! The point I was making earlier before I had to jump off. Plan your grocery list in advance to ensure you get everything you need in one trip and minimize temptations.

Maybe even use technology to spend a few minutes learning about which brands and ingredients make the best choices nutritionally speaking. With this effort, you are making good, solid, choices in your mind and pre-programming yourself with visual confirmation. Shopping with your plan and a list is helpful in avoiding the bakery or candy aisles.

Let's say you agree with yourself to get the tub of Dukes Mayo rather than whatever is on sale because it doesn't have sugar, and this is important to you now. You get there and see you could save a little on Kraft because it's on sale. This sucks you think and it's aggravating but, the Dukes label is dancing in your head. You stared at it all morning while researching ingredients and making your list so now, it's a subtle way to reinforce the power of your choices.

Also, when you're shopping, stay on the periphery of the store for the good stuff. For the most part, all the good for you stuff is on the edges of the store. When you start walking the aisles you start getting into problems.

MJ: Now I'm hungry so I'm going to make some lunch. Let's talk more about this part later.

RENEE: An excellent Idea. I would really love a salad do we have any?

End of Transcript

Figure 28: Just chillin in the deep Amazon, stumbled upon this massive vine. Oh wait is that the Ayahuasca plant? Indeed it is.

Chapter 10

Special Mention Chapter on Addiction

"I can't go back to yesterday because I was a different person then."–
Alice's Adventures in Wonderland by Lewis Carroll

In our lives, we sometimes develop habits that can turn into addictions, such as alcohol, recreational drug use, or tobacco. Some of us can honestly say they only use these things when the mood strikes or in certain situations while looking for experiences and altered states of mind. Not everyone has a "problem" with these substances. I am not, we are not doctors or therapists and addressing addictions is something we are not trained to do.

Managing your weight and health in the face of these challenges can be more difficult than most individuals anticipate. Regardless of your social circumstances, if you suspect you may have a substance use issue, it is important to seek appropriate treatment for your addiction.

There is a brave new world out there full of pioneering or experimental ways to treat addictions, deep-seated traumas and post-traumatic stress disorders which are often the root of many addictive habits. If you find yourself struggling to stop engaging in any behaviors hindering your health and well-being, I strongly recommend you to conduct thorough research on these matters independently. Psychedelics are an emerging area of interest. Studies offer a thorough understanding of their potential.

There have been experimental treatments with different mushrooms and various other plant medicines. MJ and I have a close friend named Roxy who is studying to be a Medicine Woman. She has a real love and passion for all things related to plant medicine and naturopathy. She is talented, intuitive and has the spirit of a true Shaman.

MJ and I went on a sabbatical to Peru, where we participated in Ayahuasca treatments with Roxy on two separate occasions. We were under the guidance of her trainer, a tenth generation Medicine Woman who practices plant medicine on her private land at the edge of the Amazon Jungle. Her extensive knowledge and methods have been passed down through the generations and she is the real deal. The importance of her experience and knowledge in Ayahuasca cannot be overstated enough as it is a powerful medicine. Like any strong medicine it has power to heal but like all medicine, can cause great harm if handled irresponsibly. Safety and knowledge must be researched and verified to the best of one's ability. Under no circumstances should anyone take our experience with any substance as suggested treatment, diagnosis or advice.

What I do want to impress upon you is the knowledge of its existence and how much it helped us and others close to me. Perhaps you may wish to research these alternative treatments on your own and share opinions and advice with your doctors. Finding one who will listen long enough to the possibility of benefits versus risk may be challenging but don't stop at one opinion.

Most of our pharmaceuticals today originated from plants. In fact, the main psychoactive component of Ayahuasca is not orally active on its own because it is rapidly broken down in the body by the enzyme monoamine oxidase *(MAO)*. To make Ayahuasca active when consumed orally, Ayahuasca includes another vine *(Banisteriopsis caapi.)* containing harmala alkaloids.

These alkaloids are a natural inhibitor. So what you have here is essentially an *MAOI*. Knowing this, you automatically should understand the importance of working with people who have real knowledge. Different mixes could give different results, and safety should be everyone's top priority. Having restated safety concerns and given full disclaimers, it is still plant medicine.

As our friend Roxy stated during my interview with her,

"We're at the point where weed is medicinal in many states. You can get your medical card, and you don't have to use their medical supplies. You can grow your own and the plant medicine will align with your intentions."

There's a couple of good resources online such as Erowid.org a non-profit educational resource covering many different things. Talk to one or more shamans or medicine healers and let them tell you everything they know. There is even a directory called shaman portal.org. This site provides lists of practitioners, sources for learning about plant medicine, where to obtain it, and guidance on finding legitimate providers and what plant medicines may be more suitable for you.

"I've never met anybody so powerful like this random little lady. She doesn't have any titles or certifications like on breath work or plant medicine. I asked if I could bring some people to have an Ayahuasca ceremony and she welcomed our group. She's not a retreat you know

167

because she's not trying to "sell out" to all of the commercialism happening around the plant medicine modalities. She does charge but her price is very reasonable for what she offers, she delivers the medicine, and stays with us while it's happening."

Such was my conversation with Roxy before we left for Peru. Speaking of while it's happening, I mentioned my fear and why I've always been scared to death to try psylocibins or anything more than weed. I said, "You hear things to be concerned about like bad trips." Her response was,

"Well, the real reason why bad trips even occur is because you're doing medicine in a place where you shouldn't be. You're doing medicine around people you shouldn't be around. You're not using it as medicine because this is all medicine right, and nobody's being instructed how to use it. You need the right dosage and the right setting so having any one of those out of balance is a bad trip guaranteed. They don't teach you this. Even I didn't learn this." Roxy said.

I believe many people never get an opportunity to learn about any treatments outside of the mainstream just as we don't have much opportunity to really study our food. Just as we've been insisting you should research your food and how it's handled, I would urge people to RESEARCH YOUR OPTIONS when it comes to treating addictions and know there are alternatives, particularly if you feel yours is an impossible solution.

Figure 29: I AM THE CAPTAIN!

In reality we are all our own captains in our individual journeys of life.

Chapter 11

In Closing…keep an even keel

"Either Captain Farragut would kill the narwhal, or the narwhal would kill the captain. There was no third course."– Jules Verne

Many people get locked on spending most of their life feeling shitty and overweight. Now, imagine you're taking entire flights of steps, multistory buildings of flights and doing all kinds of other wonderful things. While talking with MJ about this, we came to a few conclusions. During our conversation, she mentioned to me how she wasn't feeling good for the first time since our journey began. I reminded her how a lot of strong emotions could be triggered including fear and feelings of failure.

I told her, "You know, your body is responding in amazing ways to your new and improved choices. The fasting and weight loss have eliminated many negative factors and triggered a wave of positive changes. In my opinion, all of these shifts have set off a cascade effect within your biology. I believe these changes actually create a chemical response, sending powerful signals throughout your body. Altogether, these improvements must be creating something truly transformative within us."

It's my opinion it would have to create something like a runner's high, maybe a hormonal rush. At the opposite end of every high however, is a low. For every cresting wave, there is a trough at the bottom and you gotta go through it. You will have a drop. It will be physical, and it will be mental or emotional, and at times it might be all three. This needs to be addressed and prepared for so your drops will eventually even out before you hit bottom or ground yourself.

There will be setbacks and pitfalls. There will be runner's highs and their flip-side lows and none of us are immune to these natural cycles or universal truths. I view it as if I am a ship on the vast ocean of life, navigating as many obstacles below the surface as above. In my boat, particularly down in the bilge, it can be dirty, wet, dark, or filled with debris and failing parts. It is important to be aware of it all and perform maintenance, but spending excessive time in the bilge or revisiting the darker parts of my life may not be necessary.

As for the ocean of life well, there's so much beauty and wonder yet, also treachery and danger. When you're on top, you get sunlight and when you go down, there can be darkness all the way to the depths of despair. Our ships pilot across calm waters, rough waters and storms of different categories. What we must do on any ocean is ride the waves big and small.

So, get your equipment and charts on board. You can choose to look for and believe in reasons not to but, why fight the oceans and tides right? Instead, be fascinated by the experience of the rolling waves and take comfort in knowing that behind every low, there is always another high point, another cresting wave to triumph over. Enjoy the rocking of the ride but, paddle hard and hold your eyes steady on course even after blowing a little sideways.

MJ and I both have had to pilot these waves hard a lot lately. My metaphors are not meant to undermine or oversimplify anything. It's damn hard out here in real life but, many hands-on deck make light work and easier navigating, so I hope we have been of some service to you with these pages.

Right now, we are both experiencing a ROUGH year. We put all of our time, energy, and care into helping my dad. It has been full of the hardest, highest waves to rise atop of and the deepest of troughs to climb from in my fifty plus years of life. Our own time, self-care and habit training began to blow off course but, thankfully, we both have learned ways to prevent a total shipwreck anymore.

I mean sure, our habits slipped, and we fluctuated within a ten-to-fifteen-pound range but, we've been working our program for some time, and it feels as if when a certain set point is reached, our program reasserts itself and we get back on charted territory without too much trouble.

I think a key factor is after we spent so much time and energy working on our habits and dropping so much weight, we also dropped our bodies set point. It's as if we made our new program the default. So now, going off course means five to fifteen pounds gained rather than thirty plus. It also stretches out the length of those waves you gotta ride so your ups and downs are eventually less volatile.

Just stay awake at the helm and don't get complacent. The next time you start sliding down the other side into a deep trough, keep paddling and dig your oars in. Row a little harder. The idea is to keep your nose up high enough and headed straight into the next wave, so it rolls under your keel before you fall too deep.

If you've heard the saying "get on an even keel," your keel is that part under your boat sticking down into the water. It is a wing that flies beneath your boat and keeps you from getting all sideways, so you don't get rolled or beat down on the ocean floor. Keep your head up, face the waves and you'll eventually get on an even keel– when the height difference between the front and back end of your ship becomes less and less, the same way a teeter-totter (see-saw) stops rising and falling when both people weigh the same.

Dig deep into your waters, give it all you got because whether you like it or not, you're committed to this oceanic adventure called life, so you might as well make the best of it and get the most out of your forced participation. That's easier to do and more fun when you're healthy so you keep adjusting while the height between your trough and your next wave lessens over time. Eventually, your journey through life waves itself out into a straight line.

This year, I also experienced my first serious drop in my ability to control myself with fasting and maintaining the multiple good habits I had worked so hard on. I'd hit a plateau and wasn't showing major differences in my health, weight or body composition. My father was circling his death bed and there were more family issues to be worked out than I felt capable of handling. I was tired and stressed and gaining weight. I was in a perfect storm. Forget your waves and troughs. I had to seal the hatches, tie everything down out of my way as best I could and hold tight while the tsunami of life spun my boat over and over like an alligator in a death roll. And then…my dad called me beefy.

I would like to believe it wasn't just because dad called me beefy that I was able to right myself and get straight again. I mean, is that really all it took to give me the extra push? I thought I was more emotionally evolved. How can this still be my kryptonite and didn't I clean this out of my bilge last year? One phrase turned out to be pretty good at revving my engines full throttle. It hurt my feelings, but I remain the captain of my ship, and I will not give up. I dug deep enough and used it all to help me because you CAN'T QUIT. Be an honorable captain and don't ever abandon your own ship.

Figure 30: MJ taking a moment from yet another first in her life.

Deep Sea fishing off the coast of Jupiter Florida. Life is Amazing!

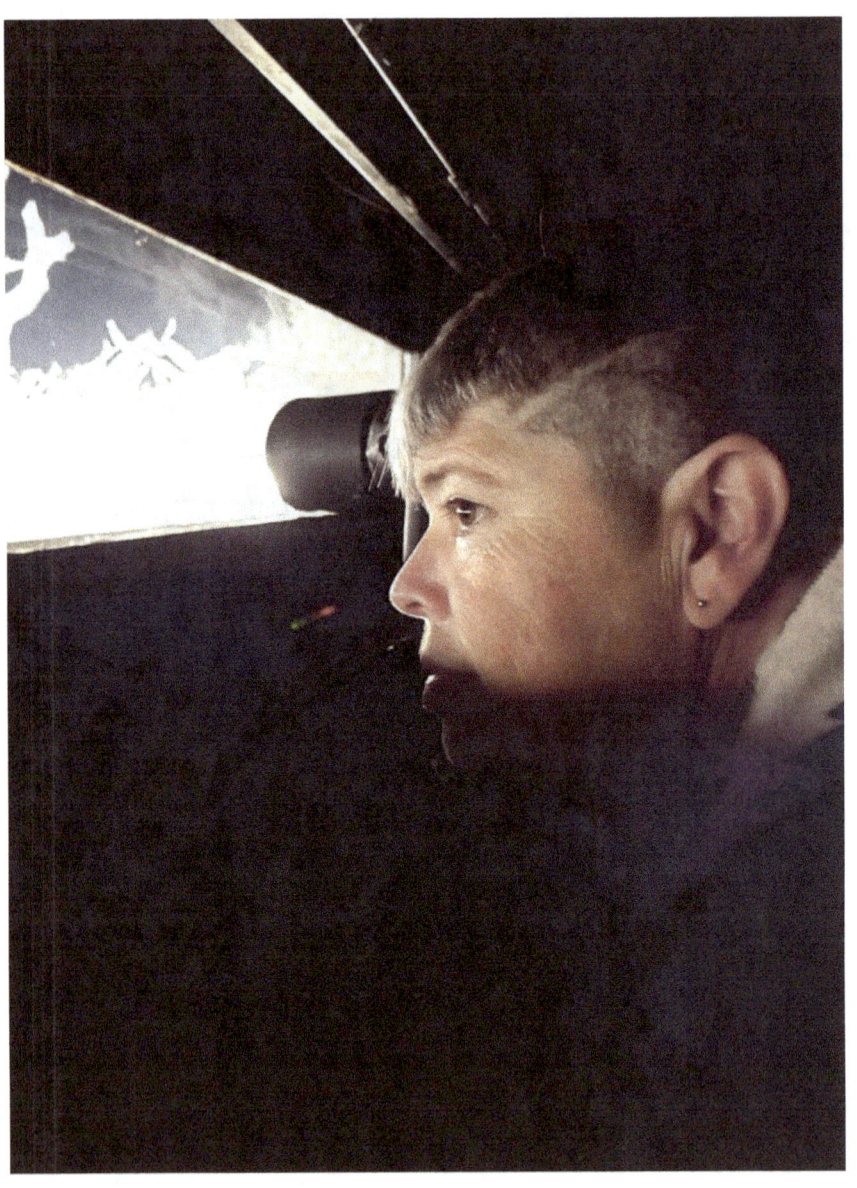

Figure 31: MJ awaiting the arrival of the local wildlife while hiding in a hide in Zimanga Africa. Another first!

Chapter 12

What now you may ask

"Are we there yet?"–

Every one, ever, who's been in the backseat

You have arrived at our last chapter but not the end of your journey or ours for that matter. There will be others, and we do plan to write all about them. For now, think of your last day of high school, remember standing outside after the last bell of your last class. Everyone has gone their separate ways to their cars, their rides, their plans and there you stand, looking at this campus which has been the center of your world for four years and now what?

Well, It's up to you. Pick one page, one piece of advice and run with it, make it your thing without fail for the next twenty-one days. Then pick another to add on and do both of those for twenty-one and forty-two days, respectively.

You came this far and all you have to do now is keep the motion, the momentum. If we helped you, don't put us down. Carry this book around with you, put it in your purse or your book bag. Find and seek out reminders that press you deeper into this newfound purpose and keep reading. Research more if you like, read some of the books suggested here or utilize the resources.

We can also give you your first assignment if that last bell rang too soon and you don't want to leave campus yet, otherwise known as Option B: Go shopping for your perfect and most amazing outfit, it could be for work, or play, every day or holiday, but it's an outfit you have longed to wear and couldn't or wouldn't because of size or shape. It should be a tad more expensive than your typical clothing budget and it should be only one or two sizes too small.

You should take pictures and print copies for posting all around you, wherever you typically spend large blocks of time. Make them big enough to capture your attention regularly. Do your homework and find out how much you must save and what weight and size you must be to look your best in this outfit. Write those answers on your prints.

Make a separate savings or a shoe box where you will deposit every dollar and cent you wanted to spend, and almost did spend on bad habits you found tempting. Each time you think of an ice-cream run, put the five or seven dollars into the savings marked "New Me" where it sits beneath the big poster of the outfit in your kitchen. If it's an electronic savings, put IOU's in your box with a running tally on the outside.

Right next to this picture of your outfit, post an equally sized print of you from earlier times in which you were smaller, you know, a picture you look back on and think, if only I were that size again. Place smaller versions of these pictures all over your life and while you're doing these things, park at the back of every lot on the opposite end of every plaza or mall.

The purpose of this exercise is to establish a small, achievable goal and to reinforce it through strong visual representation. By assigning a higher value to the goal, you can foster a sense of worth and significance while also providing yourself with a financial incentive. A photo of you weighing less is a reminder you have been here before, reinforcing it as your reality. It's a great springboard with key elements for acquiring passion and purpose.

Are we there yet? You have only just begun, but we are here to tell you, it can be one hell of an adventure and how much FUN you have with it, is up to you. Seize the day, join our email list to stay in touch. Read our bios in the next pages and get to know us, keep up with us and we look forward to your success stories. All our love and light to you and happiness only for our journeys ahead.

Warm regards, Renee & MJ.

Figure 32: Renee & MJ taking time for a photo while enjoying one of many jeep safari rides while in Zimanga Africa. Just look at that sunset!

Figure 33:Renee & MJ living life to its fullest on a boat off the coast of Jupiter Florida. Make every day an adventure!

ABOUT US - OUR BIO
POSITIVITY & PASSION

Renee:

I graduated high school– just barely. I was/am the classic under-achiever. I was always bored in school and did the bare minimum to graduate. I did however LOVE all things related to biology courses and health sciences. I also had an affinity for psychology. These courses always held my attention captive and as such, I excelled at them. I aced finals without too much studying. Sometimes I didn't study at all. I deeply regret not paying more attention to anything chemistry related since it now holds so much importance to me for food.

At 18, I joined the Army with an intent to go to college and become a doctor. War broke out and everything went on hold. After the Army, life had taken some hard turns for me, including but not limited to the fact I was going to become a single mom. At the same time, I was diagnosed with Multiple Sclerosis and told I would be in a wheelchair by 35. I was going on 22 at the time.

I hit levels of depression I didn't know existed and everything was affected. I found rock bottom and I am still alive on this planet by grace and goodwill. Things like eating well were the least of my concerns when I was trying to keep food in my son's mouth and a roof over our heads. I was using all kinds of unhealthy avenues to relieve stress and cope with my depression.

Following years of random therapy in various disciplines, many of which were paid for by charitable organizations, I began to feel how to hope and try again.

I attended a trade school specializing in the health fields. I studied anatomy and physiology for two years. I aimed for a degree, but math has always been a problem for me. I literally have trauma responses when I try to sit and study math.

A friend of mine who is a whole health practitioner gave me a book called "The Wahl's Protocol," written by Dr. Terry Wahls. I worked her program, and I began to feel better after altering my diet. Thank you Lauren, I will forever love you for that book and for your friendship over the years across many needles. The improvements were visible. My mother was also studying for a degree in alternative medicine and shared any information with me I cared to listen to. That's when I began my journey into healing myself.

When I met MJ on line, I remember thinking what a beautiful smile. Someone who smiled so openly and genuinely still had a lot of love to give herself and the world and she was asking for my help. There was never a thought to say no, and I've never looked back. As for my perspective on her beginnings, for now, let me tell you she started with one single change. She started walking. She walked every evening after dinner, every single day, sometimes two or three times a day as a new coping mechanism for stress, depression, boredom and even pain. Through arthritis pain she walked, and it helped her.

She began copying everything I did for myself. She replaced her food, her habits, and her attitude. Together we began our own long-distance training camp over video chats and hours on the phone together. The ensuing shifts in her lifestyle happened so gradually and organically she hardly missed her old ways. The new insights and perspectives she gained in those first few months were life altering because she went into this with both feet and an open mind. If I had to choose one factor for her success, I would say it was her willing and OPEN MIND. Five months later, she began experiencing new things she had always wanted to try but had been too big and unhealthy to do. She went kayaking with me.

MJ:

I was born and raised in southern Indiana. The area I grew up in was extremely rural and without many things to do. I stayed active as a child, played sports in high school and only applied myself educationally enough to stay eligible for said sports. My junior year I did apply myself to my studies with the initial intent to either go to college or join the service. Neither of these happened as life got in the way.

I spent most of my young adult days helping on a farm; I was pretty fit. By the second half of my senior year my physical appearance began to change with newly acquired bad habits and an unraveling of my own self. I have always been headstrong and stubborn, and when I realized I wasn't going to be able to pursue my initial dreams I just let myself go. I entered the workforce as a young adult working many hot strenuous days and nights in the various factories located around me. It was mainly second shift work until the wee hours of the morning.

These hours led to poor eating habits as well as a lot of alcohol consumption. It was just a matter of time before I was seeing a reflection of someone I didn't recognize staring at me in the mirror.

Being stuck in this loop, I continued to spiral downward eating and drinking myself into oblivion. This was in my twenties, you know when you're supposed to be coming up with a solid plan for the rest of your life, or at least that's what us Gen Xer's were versed on daily.

For a decade I sat idly by, wasting my life away as my once fit and toned frame became quite unrecognizable, I went from a 165-pound powerhouse to 250 pounds. My eating habits were poor. I didn't pay any attention to what I was feeding myself, my drinking was pretty out of control as well, and don't get me started on my sleep deprivation during this time in my life. It wasn't until my late twenties that I actually stepped back and took a deep look at where I was heading. It was also at this point in my life various medical conditions started to rear their ugly heads.

By 27, I was diagnosed with a severe case of ADHD and promptly placed on a stimulant. I had developed high blood pressure, bad cholesterol, and had become pre-diabetic. The medical fun didn't stop there. By 30 I was diagnosed with the auto immune disease Rheumatoid Arthritis which damn near destroyed me. Little did I know the treatments for the disease would have devastating effects on my physical and mental wellbeing for the next two decades.

I continued working to the best of my ability, supporting my family the best I could and dealing with debilitating pain day in and day out. The pain became so overwhelming I sought help with pain management, which in turn resulted in another damn pill I was being held hostage to. By the time I relocated to Florida to start my new life, I was on thirteen different pills and a weekly biological injection just to keep all that ailed me at bay.

The frame of mind I was in upon relocating to Florida was not a healthy one and I was at my heaviest ever, 350 pounds. I was in self-destruction mode with no concern for my well-being. My eighteen-year relationship had just dissolved, I sold my house, my boys were grown with family and lives of their own and I was about to embark on a journey I had intended on making when I was eighteen. Knowing my experiences in Florida wouldn't ever be what I originally hoped for, I reluctantly continued into what I felt was going to be the final chapter of my life.

That's when I met Renee. We started talking about different things, getting to know each other and she began to talk about eating and nutrition. She was so passionate about it all and it was that moment in time that everything suddenly made perfect sense. I was seeing so much clearer, so clear in fact that I caught a glimmer of my youth reflecting back through the negative hole my life had become. I asked her if she could help me and what would it take. At this point what did I have to lose? I felt I was at the bottom with no way to escape.

I don't recall the initial answer she gave me. I do know something inside of me went into hyper awareness mode. My self-destructive behaviors were put aside, and I began to focus on the help, knowledge, education, and support that Renee began to give me. The first few weeks of my journey took some serious discipline, discipline I had never displayed before in all my years.

As I sit here revisiting these moments with a heart full of gratitude yet tearing up, I'm not going to sugar coat it and say it was easy to get where I am now. I am going to say IT CAN BE DONE!!! I AM

PROOF. Over the course of the last two years, I have gone from 347 pounds all the way down to 179 pounds.

Today I have no high blood pressure, no bad cholesterol, no diabetes, and for quite some time, even my RA stayed in remission. I am planning to give my body what it needs now to heal itself further and I am no longer a slave to the pharmaceutical syndicate anymore. I have been freed of the weight of the chains of all the medications I had taken on a daily basis for many years. We are planning more travels and will be going back to the Amazon too. I am looking forward to climbing mountains.

Figure 34: Where it all began. Renee & MJ taking a break from excitement in front of the Harry Potter train station at Universal Orlando.

BIBLIOGRAPHY

1   Wang, Guijing et al. *"Annual Total Medical Expenditures Associated with Hypertension by Diabetes Status in U.S. Adults."* *American Journal of preventive medicine* (2017): S182-S189. vol. 53, 6S2.

2-8 Abramson, John. *Sickening: How Big Pharma Broke American Health Care and How We Can Repair It*. Mariner Books, 2023.

9   Siegel, Bernie S. *"Writing as Surgery: Words and Swords."* *AMA Journal of Ethics*, Journal of Ethics, 2004, journalofethics.amaassn.org/sites/journalofethics.ama-assn.org/files/2018-07/joe-0410.pdf.

10 U.S. Food and Drug Administration. (2003). *Food Additives Permitted for Direct Addition to Food for Human Consumption; Olestra*. Federal Register, 68(150), 46364-46367

11 Yang, qing, and Samuel K. Lai. *"Anti-Peg Immunity: Emergence, Characteristics, and Unaddressed Questions"* Wiley Interdisciplinary Reviews: Nanomedicine and Nanobiotechnology, vol. 7, no. 5, 2015, pp.655-677. https://doi.org/10.1002/wnan.1339

12 U.S. Government Accountability Office. *FDA Should Strengthen Its Oversight of Food Ingredients Determined to Be Generally Recognized as Safe (GRAS). GAO-10-246,* Jan. 2010. https://www.gao.gov/products/gao-10-246.

13 Reiss, Seth. *The Menu*. Searchlight Studio, 2022.

RESOURCES

Sickening
John Abramson MD MSc

The Diabetes Code
Dr. Jason Fung MD

The Wahl's Protocol
Dr. Terry Lynn Wahls MD

Guyton and Hall's Text Book of Medical Physiology
Dr. Arthur C Guyton and Dr. John E Hall

Minding My Mitochondria
Dr. Terry Lynn Wahls MD

Nurturing Your Vagus Nerve
Rachelle Escudero RN Holistic Health

https://www.drberg.com
Dr. Eric Berg DC

https://drmindypelz.com/
Dr. Mindy Pelz

https://gundrymd.com/
Dr. Steven R Gundry MD

https://www.drekberg.com/
Dr. Sten Ekberg BBA, DC

https://thomasdelauer.com/
Thomas DeLauer

https://bodyhealth.com/
Gary Brecka Mortality Modeling Expert

www.ingramcontent.com/pod-product-compliance
Lightning Source LLC
Chambersburg PA
CBHW071237130626
46556CB00003B/1055